BLIGHT OR
BLESSING

BLIGHT OR BLESSING

Managing Your Trials
as a Good Steward of God

TOM WRIGHT

XULON PRESS

Xulon Press
2301 Lucien Way #415
Maitland, FL 32751
407.339.4217
www.xulonpress.com

Unless otherwise indicated, Scripture quotations taken from the English Standard Version (ESV). Copyright © 2001 by Crossway, a publishing ministry of Good News Publishers. Used by permission. All rights reserved.

Printed in the United States of America.

Paperback ISBN-13: 978-1-6312-9490-7

Ebook ISBN-13: 978-1-6312-9491-4

Endorsements

Since trials are not just an if, but a when, we need to understand the purpose of difficult times. Tom Wright powerfully engages the reader by navigating biblically through trials to help us victoriously face the trouble of today and tomorrow.

—Jeff Beckley,
Pastoral Staff, Memorial Baptist Church, Columbus, Ohio,
Author of *Bottom Line Devotional*

"This book takes a fresh approach to the issue of suffering. Tom writes with the heart of a pastor but this Scripture rich book will challenge you at every level. Most of all, it will challenge you not just to endure but to steward your suffering for God's glory."

—Sol Green,
Retired Pastor and Biblical Counselor, Columbus, Ohio

"The test of a book's value lies in how its truths affect you. Tom Wright has written on the theme of suffering in a way that has expanded my appreciation of God's purposes in it. Suffering, particularly in the believer's life, is more than something to endure. It is a work of grace for which we will give an account as stewards. I commend Tom's book to you and trust that reading it enriches your life as much as it has mine."

—Tim Kenoyer,
Retired pastor,
Maranatha Baptist Church, Columbus, Ohio

Much has been written on trials and suffering. Getting through them, finding hope in them, conquering them...but seeing trials as stewardship and responsibility from Almighty God? What a life-altering truth! A regularly forgotten principle to an ever-relevant topic. Full of pastoral wisdom and faithful exposition, this book is packed with truth for those in trials or for those desiring to accurately and biblically care for others in the troubles of life. May the church come to comprehend the truths laid out in this work and may it be to the praise of His glory!

—Paul LaBorde,
Pastor, First Baptist Church Otsego, Michigan

"What makes a book great instead of just good is the degree to which it gives glory to God. In *Blight Or Blessing*, Pastor Wright directs our gaze upward when life hurts. Instead of asking "Why me, God?" his readers are encouraged to ask, "How can I use this trial to serve you, God?" Much of what is presented as Christian teaching today promotes the false idea that God exists to make us happy and successful. In contrast, Pastor Wright presents the biblical teaching that we exist to bring glory to God and sometimes He determines the most effective way to do that is through experiencing trials. Those who read the book and take it to heart will see their trials from a whole new perspective and begin to use their trials in a whole new way!"

—Larry Nocella,
Pastor, Camden Baptist Church, Wellington, Ohio

I happily commend Tom Wright's book on trials to you because its approach is fresh, clear, and practical. Tom writes from a warm pastoral perspective after many years of valid experience. You will be both prodded and comforted by the scriptures he deals with. He will encourage you not to 'waste your trials.'"

—Dave Warren,
Bible Conference Speaker, Friend, and Fellow Minister, Cedarville, Ohio

Dedication

To Sue, my lovely and patient wife, who by her encouragement and godly lifestyle has contributed in countless ways to the ministry and life God has called us to. I rise up and call her blessed!

Table of Contents

Acknowledgments

The Bible tells us that whatever is good and perfect comes to us from God our Father (James 1:17). God brings His gifts to us clothed in many garments—like the gift of people. I am deeply in debt to the many choice servants of God who have helped me on this journey by patiently reading the manuscript, making suggestions, offering encouragement, and going to God in prayer on our behalf.

My wife, Sue, has been my number one supporter in this work. She is patient, kind, and always ready to listen to me. She has kept me in touch with real life and reminded me of the things that are most important. She has cultivated in our home a passionate sense of gratitude to God, even in the midst of trials. I owe you, my love. I see life and our Lord better because of you! I'm so thankful to our Lord Jesus for the gift you are as my wonderful helpmate.

Our children and their spouses have also offered valuable insights that have challenged my thinking, made me laugh at myself, deepened my study, and provided much needed daily encouragement to me in the process.

I am humbled to look back on how well my parents and Sue's parents modeled the concept of "trial management" as good stewards of God. We watched them walk through severe trials with a joy and confidence rarely seen today. We have a blessed heritage that still lives on in their families.

I must express my deep appreciation for my gracious and godly father, Pastor Tom Wright Sr. (now with the Lord), my dear brother Pastor Tim Wright, our missionary friends Tom and Nancy Wolf, and our beloved friends Bob and Sylvia Will. These genuine saints of God modeled for Sue and I authentic joy and faithful stewardship of their lives and ministries in the midst of their trials. Your impact upon us is immeasurable!

Many thanks go to our MBC secretaries. Our administrative secretary, Coleen Scarberry, has invested countless hours in proof-reading, typing, revising, organizing, and coordinating this project. Our church secretary, Karen Copen, invested time and energy in cover designs and layout suggestions. Our wonderful MBC staff (Jeff Beckley and Rodney and Shelly Riley) offered suggestions and provided incredible encouragement during this process. Thank you! And the schoolteachers and authors in our church family came to my rescue many times as I sought their advice and counsel. Special thanks is due to our IT guy, Jeff Dezur, for all the great technical advice that made this task so much easier.

Many of my fellow pastors engaged with me in this experience, and their input was deeply appreciated. Thanks to Sol Green, Tim Kenoyer, Paul Laborde, Larry Nocella, and Dr. David Warren.

I owe a great deal to the friends whose books sit on my book-shelves. A vast array of God's servants, both past and present, have wisely instructed me on this journey and have helped me to understand "The Book" so much better.

My thanks also to our beloved church family, who provided the backdrop and the opportunity to test out the lessons we all learned together on this journey of trials and stewardship. What sweet and gracious people you are! I have benefitted much from your kindness to me during this exercise of writing.

I'm also deeply indebted to the Rileys for allowing me to share their story and the story of their son Joey. The hours we have spent together weeping and laughing as we have processed God's plan in trial have indelibly marked us all. I'm also very humbled and thankful for the many hours Joey and I spent together in discipleship. On the last meeting I had with him before his final deployment that would end in his death, I will never forget his words to me: "Pastor, if anything happens to me, I will be ok. Tell them I know Jesus." Little did any of us know that Joey would get to steward his trial in a way we never expected.

I am also indebted to Xulon Press and the publication team for their patience and kind input that has made this writing experience a delight.

Above all, if anything of value emerges from this project, let it be known that it is the Lord Jesus Himself that must receive the honor and praise. ! HE IS WORTHY! (Rev. 4:11).

Preface

During the course of a busy pastorate, with all that comes with caring for the flock of God (which includes the many demands of visiting, counselling, preaching, and administering the various ministries of a local church), I experienced one of those ah-hah moments you often have in ministry. In preparation for a series of messages on stewardship, as I was having my devotions in the book of Job, it dawned on me that the trials God sends into my life are part of my stewardship responsibility to Him. I never considered the struggles and difficulties which the Sovereign God introduces into my life to be stewardship opportunities. I know they are not accidents. I also know that if they are brought by God then I must learn to deal with them in His strength and for His glory. But I never considered them as a stewardship, as something given to me by God to manage as an investment for His profit.

I confess my first thought was this: "Oh, no. Another burden to carry. Something more to do. Something else to worry about. As if the trial is not enough in itself, now I have a responsibility to do something with it."

Many years ago I read Paul Billheimer's book *Don't Waste Your Sorrows,* which hinted at this very idea of trials as a stewardship. I do not claim in any way to be some kind of expert on trials in the life of a believer. I have had trials, but none near as severe as many of my brothers and sisters in Christ. At heart, I am a big chicken when it comes to trouble. I work hard at avoiding those difficulties, but I have learned that sometimes they come uninvited and always by sovereign design. I was amazed at how many men and women in the Bible managed their trials as good stewards of God. I was blind to this approach to trials for a long time.

I began to ask myself the following questions: What if trials are part of God's plan to teach me stewardship of all He has given me? What if trials are the basis upon which God chooses to bring great reward into my life? What if trials help me understand more of His will, His Word, and His wonder than any other vehicle He could use at that moment in my life? What if trials are part of the good gifts and perfect gifts James speaks of that are sent from our Heavenly Father? And what if, in learning to manage them as a good steward of God (of course with His strength undergirding me, for I have little of my own to do this) I discover that what started out as some kind of blight on my life, ended up in unexpected blessing?

After preaching the series of studies I had prepared on this subject, I was surprised and a bit shocked at all the requests I received for copies of the messages. Many have encouraged me to put them into print so others could benefit from the truth of God's Word on the subject trials and stewardship. I'm not a professional, but a simple pastor who loves his people and who needed these messages perhaps more than anyone else.

Whether you are a new believer or a mature believer, a seminary graduate or just trained in your own local church, it is my prayer that this book will encourage you to embrace your trials as a stewardship and find in them a source of blessing instead of crushing blight in your life.

Soli Deo Gloria!
Tom Wright

Foreword

Question: "When are you going to write a book, Dad?"
Response: "What would I write about that anyone would
want to read?"

The dad in this exchange is the author of the book you're
holding in your hand. The question was asked many times,
over many years by various members of his family, including the
author himself. Why did we all think he was a good candidate for
writing a book? The simple answer is that he has accumulated a lot
of wisdom over the years—wisdom worth sharing. The reason for
this is His love for the Word of God, which has characterized his
entire adult life. Biblical truth seems to ooze out of him like jelly
from a squeezable jar.

One of the topics he has addressed repeatedly during his fif-
ty-plus years of pastoral ministry is the trials of life. The shepherd
of a church usually doesn't have to wait very long before the next
trial comes along to one of the members of his flock. When it does,
he comes alongside that individual or family offering both comfort
and counsel. Pastor Wright has brought the comfort and counsel
of Scripture to people in the trials of life as they sat across from his
desk in his study, laid in a hospital bed, or stood by the graveside
of a loved one. His message almost always included the reminders

that God loved and cared about them and promised not to abandon them in their time of trial.

He would also remind them that God has a plan and purpose for everything that happens in their lives, even if they don't understand it and that their responsibility is to continue to trust Him. He would be sure to include the fact that Jesus Christ, God's Son experienced the ultimate trial of taking on the sin of the whole world and enduring the wrath of God in order to pay for their sin. Pastor Wright would share these biblical truths with hurting people because that's what a good pastor does.

But a good pastor does more than just remind people of what they already know. He is constantly striving to grow in the grace and knowledge of our Lord and Savior Jesus Christ (2 Pet. 3:18) himself and help others do the same. Pastor Wright's growth in the knowledge of Jesus Christ, as taught in the Bible, led him to the understanding that God wants His people to view the trials in their lives in a way that most Christians probably never even thought of before. He began to see and understand the biblical teaching of stewardship in the area of trials. This involves viewing trials just as you would any other resource God entrusts to you. It is one thing to accept what God allows in your life. It is quite another thing to count it all joy when you encounter various trials. Still, beyond either of these is the ability to see your trials as unique opportunities to glorify God even as they are unfolding. It is this last category that explores the idea of stewarding our trials. Pastor Wright points out just how truly biblical this concept is even though it is a novel thought to most Christians.

In the classic play *Fiddler on the Roof*, the main character, Tevye, struggles through the trials of life unique to being a Jew living in Russia in the early 1900s. He has an ongoing, one-sided conversation with God, wondering why he has to suffer through poverty, pogroms, struggling to complete his daily milk deliveries with a lame horse, having five daughters but no sons to assist him in his work, etc. He concludes that the coping mechanism God has given him and his people to help deal with all these trials is tradition. Tradition is what Jewish people hang onto when everything else around them falls apart. Never does it occur to Tevye that the trials themselves are not only from God but provide a unique opportunity to serve God. Sadly, this idea rarely occurs to many Christians, as well. That is why this book is so needed.

The author became my father-in-law almost three decades ago. Before that, he was my pastor. I have watched him shepherd people through the trials of life. I have also watched him go through some of his own, always relying on God for strength to get through it and using them to point people to Christ. What he writes about is not simply the result of his studies but rather the result of his study of the Scripture lived out and put into practice. My hope is that you too will see that God wants you to steward the trials of life He sends your way.

Larry Nocella
March 2020

Introduction

Trials as a Stewardship

Stewardship is not a word we commonly associate with trials. If you're like me, when you hear the word *stewardship*, you think of money or resources. Yet the very word suggests a wider meaning. Stewardship is simply the managing of someone else's property. You can have good stewardship or bad stewardship.

Think of it like this. If you loan me your car and I return it all dinged up, I've been a bad steward of your property. But if I return your car in good shape, I would be considered a good steward.

Paul speaks of his ministry of preaching the Gospel as a stewardship in Titus 1:2–3:

"In hope of eternal life, which God, who never lies, promised before the ages began and at the proper time manifested in his word through the preaching with which I have been entrusted by the command of God our Savior."

The word *entrusted* is a stewardship word.

Paul also speaks of Timothy's ministry battles as a stewardship when he says, in 1 Timothy 1:18–19, "This charge I entrust to you Timothy...that you may wage the good warfare, holding faith and a good conscience..."

Staying true to God's Word and keeping his conscience clear was to be understood as Timothy's stewardship responsibilities.

Let's not forget Paul's account of the Macedonians' stewardship. He challenged the Corinthians to emulate their example of stewardship when he said, in 2 Corinthians 8:5, "But they gave themselves first to the Lord and then by the will of God to us."

There is no doubt that the entire life of a believer in Christ is to be understood as a stewardship. Stewardship goes way beyond just our money and resources. This includes our ministries and even our bodies. The way we use our minds and bodies will be brought into account because they are God's property and we must learn to steward them wisely in His will.

"Or do you not know that your body is a temple of the Holy Spirit within you, whom you have from God? You are not your own, for you were bought with a price. So glorify God in your body" (1 Cor. 6:19–20).

The beloved English preacher W. E. Sangster, when he was diagnosed with progressive muscular atrophy, realized this trial would eventually take his life. At that time he composed four rules for himself to help him be a good steward of his trial:

> "I will never complain. I will keep the home bright. I
> will count my blessings. I will try to turn it to gain."[1]

The problem with trials is that they can be viewed as a blight on life. In botany, for instance, a blight is a disease or injury of plants marked by the formation of lesions, withering, and the death of parts. A blight is also something that frustrates plans or hopes, like an abandoned factory spoken of as a blight on the neighborhood. So when we think of a blight, we connect it with something that impairs or destroys. Is that how we must approach the idea of our trials—as just a blight on our lives? After all, I've never heard anyone say, "Hey, my trials are a blast. So much fun!"

C. S. Lewis likened suffering and trials to sitting in a dentist chair:

> "It doesn't really matter whether you grip the arms of the dentist's chair or let your hands lie in your lap. The drill drills on."[2]

Is it possible, however, to view trials as a blessing? Can a trial ever be a thing conducive to joy or beneficial welfare? Can a trial ever encourage us or be a sign of God's favor and protection toward us? Can a trial become a vehicle for reward and a door for greater experiences? Can a trial in real and practical terms actually produce blessing?

And, let's face it, who does not have trials in this fallen world? If we're to benefit from our trials and navigate them successfully by God's design, we must learn what it means to "steward" our trials, viewing them and their effects as God's property. Because they're happening to me by the design and will of God then I must

Trials are actually my assignment!

come to look at my trials as His work in me and even His work through me for the blessing of others. Trials are actually my assignment! Managing that work of God in me and through me calls for understanding the basics of an all-life stewardship. In the real grit of life is it possible to actually think like that and live like that? Is this part of my God-given assignment?

On this little journey together, we'll examine Paul's writings on trials and stewardship from 2 Corinthians 4, 5, and 8. Then we'll take a look at how James connects trials and stewardship (James 1). We will consider Peter's focus on trials and stewardship (1 Pet.

1). We will conclude by putting "faces" on trials, as we observe how Hannah and Job managed their trials as good stewards of God.

It's my goal that you will not find being a good steward of your trials to be a burdensome task—a blight—but a freeing, encouraging, and life-altering experience that becomes blessing. God strengthens us for such an assignment and we will learn together how to draw on that strength.

Chapter One

Clay Pot Living:
2 Corinthians 4

Let's suppose I have a clay flowerpot. We've all seen them. These pots are not worth much. They are certainly not anything to write home about. They're rather common and ordinary and hardly worth a second look. They're useful for putting things in, but they won't last a long time because they're subject to being easily broken, cracked, and weathered.

In fact, if a thief were to break into my house, he wouldn't say to his buddy, "Hey, look, there's a clay flowerpot. Let's grab that. We can make some real money on that." No, I can pretty much guarantee that this pot will be left behind and overlooked.

But there's something they don't know. I have put something very valuable inside this cheap thing.

The Bible tells us that we are like clay pots, but not just any clay pots. We're told that we have a treasure in this vessel of clay. To understand this concept, let's take a look at my old clay flowerpot again.

Suppose I were to offer this clay pot to a young boy. And suppose I were to put a hundred-dollar bill in the pot as a treasure. I would show the pot and the "treasure" (my hundred-dollar bill) to this boy. Then I might pose some questions to him and the conversation might go something like this:

Me: Whose clay pot is this?

Boy: Yours.

Me: Right. Whose treasure is this?

Boy: Yours.

Me: Right again. Hey, you're a good student. Would you like to have this hundred-dollar bill?

Boy: Wow! You bet I would.

Me: I thought you might say that. Well, it is connected to the clay pot. You have to take them both. Tell you what. I'm going to give you the pot and its treasure. But you have to remember two things after I give them to you. Here is the first thing. This pot will still be mine. OK?

Boy: OK.

Me: Now whose is it?

Boy: Yours.

Me: I am going to let you use it for me. But here is what I want you to do with it. I want you to take care of the pot. You can put a flower in it, you can store stuff in it. You can decorate it, paint it, put stickers on it, glitter it up in any way you might think I would like.

Boy: OK

Me: Here's the second thing I want you to remember. There's the matter of this treasure. It's mine too but I want you to use it. I want you to put some of it in the offering next week. Now you don't have to, but it is mine and that is what I want you to do with it. How much you put in is up to you.

Boy: Cool!

Me: The rest of the treasure I want you to enjoy. Don't use it for anything that will hurt you or others. But you can spend it on anything you would like and enjoy. OK? Good deal huh?

Boy: That sure is. Can I have it now?

Me: Of course. Oh, one more thing. Someday I am going to ask what you did with my pot and my treasure. Not next week, or maybe not even next month, but I will ask you—in front of everybody—what you did with my pot and my treasure. OK. Are we clear?

Boy: Yeah, sure.

Me: Well, have a good day.

You see, our stewardship is lived out in front of God. Someday, He is going to ask us what we did with His treasure. The clay pot is going to get some life bruises on it called trials. God wants us to manage those trials because inside of us there is something very valuable. Of course, if you have not guessed, the treasure is Christ Himself dwelling in us.

In 2 Corinthians 4, Paul likens the life and body of a believer to a simple clay jar, not just any clay jar, but one that houses a rich treasure.

Here he is writing to a church about two vital concerns he has for them. He wants them to learn how to grow strong and to stay faithful. Paul uses his team as an example to the church of both growing strong and staying faithful in ministry. But Paul is not naïve about the challenges this will present for us. Clay pots have problems.

The Problems with Clay Pot Living

Paul recognized that there some very real problems that come with living in clay jars. Managing our trials in this clay pot will not be easy.

> "We all have a Gethsemane—that is, a place and time in our lives when we face sorrow on the deepest level—a place of crisis, grief, anguish, excruciating pain, and loss. It's a time of separation, a tearing, or the ending of a relationship with

someone or something that causes us to stop in our spiritual tracks and look more closely at who we are, our circumstances, and those around us. It brutally exposes what we honestly believe to be true in regard to God and His Word."[3]

Clay pot living is a life of trials and problems. And those problems can be daunting for us. As most of us have learned the coronavirus pandemic highlighted the frailty of our clay vessels. With all of our technology and advanced medical science, we found ourselves fighting to patch up and keep the clay jars intact. The Governor of New York, Andrew Cuomo, likened the COVID-19 virus to being in one of those snow globes, where someone turned it upside down, shook it real hard, and turned it back over again. As a result, we were left overwhelmed and didn't know what to do.

It is to the Word of God we must go for relief and comfort in the midst of such clay pot challenges, whether they be global or personal.

In 2 Corinthians 4:1–4, Paul says, "Therefore, having this ministry by the mercy of God, we do not lose heart. But we have renounced disgraceful, underhanded ways. We refuse to practice cunning or to tamper with God's Word, but by the open statement of the truth we would commend ourselves to everyone's conscience in the sight of God. And even if our gospel is veiled, it is veiled only to those who are perishing. In their case the god of this world has blinded the minds of the unbelievers, to keep them from seeing the light of the gospel of the glory of Christ, who is the image of God."

Did you hear Paul mention all those clay pot problems? Let's look at some of them.

Problem One: Losing Heart

According to 2 Corinthians 4:1, there is the "losing heart" kind of problem. That's another way of expressing being down and discouraged.

Tim Keller relates how his father toward the end of his life, suffering with many ailments and was deeply discouraged. A friend of his encouraged his father during this time with the following:

> "Jesus was patient under even greater suffering for us,
> so we can be patient under lesser suffering for him
> (Heb. 12:3–4). And heaven will make amends for
> everything."[4]

Earlier in 2 Corinthians 1:8 Paul confessed that he and his team did struggle with the severe trials afflicting them. Yet here, just a few chapters later, he gives us a few of the reasons why they were able to stay encouraged (4:13–15).

Reason # 1: Even though they did not deny the reality of what was happening to them (they were not in denial), they could speak realistically about their trial. Why? Because they believed the word of God with the same kind of faith that the Psalmist expressed.

"Since we have the same spirit of faith according to what was been written, "I believed, and so I spoke, we also believe, and so we also speak" (4:13).

The psalmist confessed God had delivered his soul from death, his eyes from tears, and his feet from stumbling, enabling him to walk before the Lord in this life with all its trials and afflictions. He believed and was comforted by all God's benefits that came to him (Ps. 116:8–14). And that is what Paul and his team believed as well. Thus, they did not lose heart.

Reason # 2: They knew that a resurrection was coming (4:14). Their confidence in the future, based on Christ's resurrection in the past, undergirded them and kept the "boogey man" of discouragement from beating down their door. The hope of the resurrection—the idea that we are headed for a good outcome in spite of what we are facing today—infuses our spirit with hope and comfort. It did that for Paul and his team and it will do the same for us. We must not lose heart.

The next time you have an occasion to go to a cemetery, remember that some of those gravestones hide a resurrection body. We call the cemetery a final resting place. Not so! There is coming a resurrection for all—some to everlasting life, and some to shame and everlasting contempt (Dan. 12:2).

Reason # 3: They knew their suffering was benefitting the church and glorifying God (4:15). The grace that they were receiving was being felt by others and it was leading to a chorus of thanksgiving and praise to God. As we live life in our clay jar on the stage of trials, we may not see all that God is doing to benefit others in the body of Christ. To be used as a servant of God and bring to light the treasure that is in us is indeed a rare privilege. Our trials amount to something for good in the lives of others and it brings God the glory He so rightfully deserves. So let's not lose heart.

> *It is easy to forget that everything we have been given and enjoy comes because of God's mercy and grace to us.*

Maybe it is time for a little grace exercise. Paul speaks about grace extending to more and more (4:15). It is easy to forget that everything we have been given and enjoy comes because of God's mercy and grace to us. Losing heart in trial often stems back to our short and shallow view of grace. Our privileges as well as our opportunities to serve the Lord all come by God's grace. There is no merit system when it comes to mercy and grace. We were brought in by grace. And we will be carried home by grace. "Surely goodness and mercy shall follow me all the days of my life" (Ps. 23:6). What makes us lose heart is when we blot out the thought of God's grace and begin to think that we have what we have or should have what we want because we earned it or deserved it. Paul said bluntly, in 1 Corinthians 15:10, "But by the grace of God I am what I am, and His grace toward me was not in vain. On the contrary, I worked harder than any of them, though it was not I, but the grace of God that is with me."

Let's make this practical. Take the matter of prayer. Have you ever prayed for God to give you something or spare you from something and God did not do it? When we lose sight of our status as a child of God, and forget that we are recipients of God's great and wonderful grace, we can begin to pray like religious people, not God's children. Our prayers take on a business-relationship format, and we forget grace.

Recently, a man shared with me that he hadn't seen God answer any of his prayers in a long time. I asked him why he thought that was true. He answered because he did not get what he hoped for. I challenged him to think about the father/child relationship he has with God. Like an earthly father does not grant all the requests of his children because he knows many of those requests are not wise, so it is with our Heavenly Father. On the other hand, God may answer the prayer very differently than I imagine. I may miss seeing his "better" answer because I'm too determined that God see things my way. It may also be true that God is working on me through His Spirit and His word to reveal some sin in me or to bring some changes in my life so that the answers to my prayers come into a life that is ready for them.

When we realize we're His children through His grace and mercy in Christ, we can then approach God in a way that's natural to a father-child relationship. This is a trusting relationship that will continue to breed a healthy prayer life.

John Freeman, in his book *Hide or Seek*, put it this way:

> "Prayer is not a magic incantation to achieve a desired result or the right sequence of buttons on a vending machine that will yield the snack you crave. Prayer is a conversation that allows a Father to help shape the character of His son."[5]

Jeremiah had it right in Lamentations 3:23–24 when he said, "Because of the steadfast love of the Lord we are not cut off [lit.], His mercies never come to an end, they are new every morning, great is your faithfulness."

Problem Two: Self-Promotion

Another problem we're likely to face is the promote-yourself kind of problem. This is where we make "us" the center of all that's happening in life. That's why Paul warns us in 2 Corinthians 4:2 that we are stewards, not owners. To be trustworthy implies that we have the owner's best interests at heart, not our own. A steward cannot be self-serving and still be a good steward.

Will Rogers used to say,

> "I always like to hear a man talk about himself because then I never hear anything but good."[6]

Trials can easily put us on the defensive by leading us to think only of ourselves and the unfairness of life to us. Someone said that a bore is a man who spends so much time talking and thinking about himself that you can't talk about yourself.

Awhile back I was tasked with counseling a young couple regarding some marriage conflicts that were derailing their relationship. As I sat and listened to the defenses of their own righteous behavior and the perceived miscues of their spouses, it dawned on me how many times I was hearing the word *I*. *I* felt like this. *I* was offended by that. *I* needed this. And on the conversation went. Finally, I graciously (I hope it was gracious) brought their me-ism dialogue to an end. For the rest of our time we talked about the issue of self-promotion and self-interest. Each of them had moved into the center of the relationship in which there was only room for one. There was no elbow room allowed in the center, because each of them wanted to hog the spotlight of their relationship. When we examined the model of Christ with his church (Eph. 5:22–33), and considered carefully the character of Jesus in Philippians 2:5–8, the walls started to fall. I am happy to report that this couple today now walk in harmony very conscious of the dangers that self-will, self-promotion, and self-interest pose to their marriage relationship.

Trials can make selfish little dudes out of us all if we are not careful. It's easy to centralize ourselves and play pity party all day long. But it's not about us. It never has been. Paul got it right when he said in Col. 1:16-17: "—all things were created through him and <u>for him</u> (Christ). And he is before all things, and in him all things hold together."

Problem Three: Other People

Paul talks about the problem of people too (2 Cor. 4:3–4). You will often face unresponsive people, namely, people who refuse to listen to your testimony and witness about Christ. People may also lay the blame for your trial at your feet. And it is just here that they can easily derail your stewardship. We can depend too much on people for affirmation and support. And when it's not forthcoming, we can become disillusioned and bitter.

Now we are not to think that community in the body of Christ provides nothing for us in trial. After all, we are told that every person in the body of Christ has a gift and function that we all need. We cannot say we do not need one another, neither can we isolate ourselves and live our clay jar life like some kind of "lone ranger," independent of those God has placed around us (1 Cor. 12).

However, there comes a time when human support and help falls far short (Jer. 17:5–6). Paul experienced this when he faced people who had falsely judged his team and as a result refused his testimony.

Being under fire and deeply hurt by the accusations and criticisms of others is not an easy thing to endure. These false teachers claimed Paul and his team were after money, pride of position, and many other false notions. Certainly the false teachers in Corinth were characterized by such practices. Now many people would have crumbled in the face of such treatment, but Paul managed these trials as a good steward.

I remember counseling an individual who constantly worried that he'd made bad financial choices, which he believed were catching up with him. He was undergoing a severe financial trial and many of his acquaintances accused him of mismanagement and unwise choices. Sometimes that's true. Many people do reap consequences of unwise financial choices. However, in this case the true reality was that this man had actually practiced good stewardship and had made many wise choices. The circumstances of the trial were thrust upon him through no fault of his own. Yet many misjudged him. I reminded him that God punished Jesus for his sins and God is not exacting a pound of flesh from him in this trial. We must let God bring out our righteousness before others in His own way and time (Ps. 37:6).

Paul's enemies, wrongly concluded, that his suffering was evidence that God was displeased with him and he was reaping the consequences of his "mistakes."

However, Paul looked at those same sufferings as authenticating his apostleship, and giving him a sign of God's favor upon him. Luke tells us that suffering was part of Paul's original call and mission: "But the Lord said to him, 'Go, for he is a chosen instrument of mine to carry my name before the Gentiles and kings and the children of Israel. For I will show him how much he must suffer for the sake of my name'" (Acts 9:15–16).

These sufferings did highlight Paul's own weakness, but they also made room for God's power to work in and through his weakness, enabling him to fulfill the mission God had given him.

In a very similar way Peter reminds us that our own calling as believers will involve suffering for Jesus' sake.

"For to this you have been called, because Christ also suffered for you, leaving you an example, so that you might follow in his steps" (I Pet. 2:21).

We are expected to manage these trials as Jesus did.

"He committed no sin, neither was deceit found in his mouth. When he was reviled, he did not revile in return; when he suffered, he did not threaten but continued entrusting himself to him who judges justly" (I Pet. 2:22–23).

Problem Four: Our Mission

Paul understood that the way he handled his trials would impact his mission. This is a real problem. Notice what he says in 2 Corinthians 4:5–6:

"For what we proclaim is not ourselves, but Jesus Christ as Lord, with ourselves as your servants for Jesus' sake. For God, who said,

"Let light shine out of darkness," has shone in our hearts to give the light of the knowledge of the glory of God in the face of Jesus Christ."

Our mission is to light up the darkness of this world even in the midst of trial. We are to do this in two ways:

First, we must proclaim Christ not ourselves (4:5a). Christ is our message and in spite of our trials, we must continue to seek ways to stay on mission. This clay pot life must be one of Christ conscious living, not self-conscious living.

> "Sometimes God permits our vessels to be jarred so that some of the treasure will spill out and enrich others."[7]

Secondly, we must live as servants to others (4:5b). We are to continually find ways to help and serve others for Jesus' sake. Paul reminded the Corinthians that they were letters of recommendation to be known and read of all men (3:2).

Proclaiming Christ and living as His servants epitomizes trial stewardship that needs to be read by all men.

Edward Judson, son of the famous missionary Adoniram Judson, put this into perspective:

> "Success and suffering are vitally and organically linked. If you succeed without suffering, it is because someone else has suffered before you; if you suffer without succeeding, it is that someone else may succeed after you."[8]

Let me tell you the story of Rodney and Shelly Riley. The Rileys have served as music director and wife in our church fellowship for several years. On November 24, 2014, they received the news no parent wishes to receive. Their youngest son, Joey, was killed when

12

a vehicle-borne improvised explosive device struck his vehicle in Afghanistan. The news was devastating to them and to us as a church family. Now Joey knew Jesus Christ as his Savior and made his testimony clear to the men he served with in the army. We all rejoice in the wonderful reality that Joey is with Christ—yet that assurance does not make the trial go away. Joey received many awards as one of the top sniper soldiers in his unit. His awards and decorations included the Bronze Star Medal, Purple Heart, Army Commendation Medal, Army Achievement Medal, Afghanistan Campaign Medal with campaign star, Global War on Terrorism Service Medal, Army Service Ribbon, Overseas Service Ribbon, NATO medal, Combat Infantryman Badge and Basic Parachutist Badge.

But the real story of Joey's life happened after his death. His mother and father determined that they would steward their trial for the sake of the Gospel. They have spoken at many public events about the power of the Gospel in their son's life and in their own lives personally. Has it been easy? Do they still grieve at times? The answer is yes to both of those questions. Has this life stewardship of their trials made any difference? The answer is also a resounding yes. At Joey's funeral thousands lined the streets of their town. Hundreds crowded into the church for the memorial service. Over and over the Gospel story was shared by Joey's parents. The newspapers, radio, and TV stations in central Ohio all carried the story with the text of the memorial message I had the privilege of giving. Interview after interview, from the governor of the state of Ohio, the mayor, senators, representatives, news media, to conversations with people on the street—all heard the Gospel. But there is more. Through the faithful prayers and witness of Joey's parents in their trial, Joey's uncle recently came to faith in Christ. Joey's best friend who served right alongside him in the army recently came to faith in Christ and was baptized, all as a result of Joey's parents praying for him and sharing the Gospel with him from Joey's story. And the story continues. Almost every day the Rileys find opportunity to share the Gospel and do so with joy behind their tears. Is their trial a blight or a blessing? They chose blessing.

When we are going through trials the hardest thing to do is to keep serving. And yet it is our mission. Serving is one way we handle our trials. And Paul says we are to do it for Jesus' sake.

Warren Wiersbe challenges us not to give up too easily:

"When your service is the most difficult, God may
be doing His deepest work in you."[9]

Let's think about this. If we continue to serve when it is difficult, the deep work of God will be to bring to the forefront of our lives Jesus Christ. God wants men to see the light in us, which is Christ. The darkness of my trial is a perfect background for the glorious light of Christ. Remember the day Jesus healed the man who was blind from birth? Jesus explained to his disciples that this man's trial was for the sole purpose of displaying the works of God in him (John 9:3).

That's why it is God's desire that everything we do be for Jesus' sake.

"For what we proclaim is not ourselves, but ourselves as your servants for Jesus' sake." (2 Cor. 4:5).

God's goal is that Jesus Christ receive the preeminence in all of human life and behavior. Why? Because all things were created through him and for Him. (Col. 1:15–18).

It's because of God's goal to proclaim Christ and serve others that the darkness has any hope of being lifted.

"For God, who said, 'Let light shine out of darkness to give the light..." (2 Cor. 4:6a).

We can only light up the world because Christ, Who is the light, lives in us. We serve by giving others the light. We un-cloud the lenses of our lives by seeking the good of others for Jesus's sake (2 Cor. 4:5).

One of Paul's trials while on a journey aboard a ship gives us a picture of what this looks like. Paul stays on mission during a terrible storm that ended with a shipwreck. This scene unfolds in Acts 27. Paul is a prisoner on the way to Rome, because he has appealed to Caesar. A dangerous storm emerges and the ship is in trouble. It ultimately sinks, but all on board are spared and make it out alive onto an island. Now they make it out alive because Paul stayed on mission, bringing light to the sailors and crew as well as the other prisoners. What kept the trial from overwhelming him?

First, Paul trusted the One who possessed him in this stormy circumstance. He said that an angel of the God to whom he belonged stood with him (Acts 27:24–25). He who has called us is the one to whom we belong as well.

F. B. Meyer, in his book *The Gift of Suffering*, reflects Paul's mind-set at this moment in his life:

> "He looked on the storm, and he said: 'This is my Father's world; this dark night, it is my Father's; and I am His child, and He loves me too well to forget me. I am His. The God who made this foaming ocean is my Father; The God who lets those winds blow forth is my God; all this world is but a mansion—my Father's house. And I am safe because my Father rules the Storm."[10]

This trial impacted his mission for good, because he managed it as a good steward.

Adoniram Judson, the renowned missionary to Burma, endured untold hardships trying to reach the lost for Christ. For seven heartbreaking years he suffered hunger and privation. During this time he was thrown into Ava Prison, and for seventeen months was subjected to almost incredible mistreatment. As a result, for the rest of his life he carried the ugly marks made by the chains and iron shackles which had cruelly bound him. Undaunted, upon his release he asked for permission to enter another province where he might resume preaching the Gospel. Judson decided to manage his trials as a good steward of God in service to others for the sake of the Gospel. But the godless ruler indignantly denied his request, saying,

> "My people are not fools enough to listen to anything a missionary might say, but I fear they might be impressed by your scars and turn to your religion!"[11]

Oh, the power of a well-managed trial for the sake of Christ. Judson knew to whom he belonged.

There was a second thing that prevented Paul from becoming overwhelmed and "throwing overboard" his mission during those moments. Paul trusted the Word of God. He simply believed what God said:

"And he said, 'Do not be afraid, Paul; you must stand before Caesar. And behold, God has granted you all those who sail with you.' So take heart, men, for I have faith in God that it will be exactly as I have been told" (Acts 27:24–25).

Paul and the Psalmist of old stood on the same ground:

"Your word is a lamp to my feet and a light to my path...I am severely afflicted; give me life, O LORD, according to your word!" (Ps. 119:105, 107).

Paul was a light to those men. He served them in the midst of the trial that came upon him. He stayed on mission in the trial because he had unshakable confidence in the Word of the living God, and so must we.

Trials can't be dismissed or excluded from our mission as if they don't matter. They do matter because trials impact our mission of serving others and lifting up our Savior for all to see. And the Word of God is the key to our confidence as it was for Paul.

Recently a man came to me seeking input on his doctoral dissertation from a seminary in the Midwest. He had written a book that was to be part of his dissertation requirement and asked if I would respond to the synopsis and underlying argument of the book. Much of his foundation for his views were drawn from his own visions and dreams he claimed to have received from the Holy Spirit. His dissertation advanced the theory that God will save some of the lost in the afterlife and that Christians who do not strive to obey Christ here will need purification in the afterlife. As a result, his conclusion advances the idea that churches should reform their faith statements to identify God's sovereignty in the afterlife. As I explained his misunderstanding of the atonement of Christ, and the flaw in believing that there is open revelation today, my heart went out to him, for I saw a man who was sincere but misguided. What happened at the end of our conversation was both amazing and sobering. I asked him how I could pray for him. He shared some great struggles he was enduring and doubts he was wrestling with. I took the Bible and shared a couple of passages that I thought would open his eyes to the great power and wonder of Christ when we are undergoing the rough moments of life. After I prayed, he said that he had never really heard the truth of what I shared with him before. It was my joy to point out that the Word of God is not a textbook but a living revelation, and a powerful double-edged sword (Heb. 4:12) given to reveal God's will and comfort to us in a way nothing else can. I pray

> *Never underestimate what the Word of God can do in our trials.*

that in his trial the Word of God will become real and that Christ will be seen for who He really is and what He came to do.

Never underestimate what the Word of God can do in our trials.

Problem Five: God's Plan

Living in a clay jar means coming to the realization that trials are part of God's plan. Paul explains that trials come with the territory of confessing and serving Christ.

This is no accident. It's a planned thing.

"For we who live are always being given over to death for Jesus' sake, so that the life of Jesus also may be manifested in our mortal flesh (2 Cor. 4:11).

Let's explore this planned-trial thing a little bit. God uses a little word to encompass the scope of our trials when he tells us to "count it all joy when we face trials..." (James 1:2). The "it" refers to our trials. This little word *it* contains the whole thing. *It* sums up in its tiny footprint every one of the various trials we have. *It* speaks of trials which the present may contain or trials which the future may bring or even trials which the past may keep stored up in our memories.

God also uses a simple word to teach us that trials are unavoidable when He says, "When you meet trials..." The word *meet* suggests inevitability. Some translations use the words falling *upon* or *into*. This word is used in Acts 27:41 in a nautical setting: "But striking a reef, they ran the vessel aground. The bow stuck and remained immovable, and

Life is full of those hidden rocks, and sudden violent winds of circumstances lying in wait for us as believers.

the stern was being broken up by the surf." Paul's experienced sailors did not plan to strike a reef for they did not know it was there—but they did strike it. That's our verb *meet*.

18

There is an inevitability about our trials that comes from living in a fallen world. There is also an inevitability about the trials of a follower of Christ, because identity with Christ will bring out the animosity of the world against them (John 15:18–25).

Let's face it. Life is full of those hidden rocks, and sudden violent winds of circumstances lying in wait for us as believers.

Now think about this. Is the *it* random, arbitrary, or accidental? Or is something more significant going on when *it* comes knocking? Is the *meeting* of a trial experience an exception to the rule in our lives, or is it something to be expected? Is there a plan afoot or is *it* brought on by the winds of fate?

J. A. Motyer, in his little book on James observes,

> "There is no trial, no great calamity or small pressure,
> no overwhelming sorrow or small rub of life outside
> that plan of God."[12]

If it is true that God's plan for me includes trial, then the problem I inevitably face is this: Is there any God-given and practical resource available to help me weather this trial experience that's part of His plan? We have a wonderful and practical tool God longs to put in our toolbox. Clay pot living desperately needs this tool.

The Tool of Wisdom

God has wisely provided for us the tool of His wisdom, direction and counsel to manage and navigate our trials as good stewards.

"If any of you lacks wisdom, let him ask God, who gives generously to all without reproach, and it will be given him. But let him ask in faith, with no doubting, for the one who doubts is like a wave of the sea that is driven and tossed by the wind. For that person must not suppose that he will receive anything from the Lord; he is a double-minded man, unstable in all his ways. Let the lowly brother boast in his exaltation..." (James 1:5–9)

Be assured that God's plans for us do not put us into a position of bare existence. We may not have what we want, but we will have what we need. We are people who need not fear that our trials will do us in. We have "stuff," that comes from knowing Christ. Nothing points out your lack of knowledge like being given a task you don't know how to perform. It may be just a simple of lack of tools. In my case it is more likely the lack of experience or know-how to complete the job. Take plumbing issues in the house. When I end up needing to replace toilet seals or faucet washers, etc., I trot off to the computer, go to good old YouTube and search for my problem. Now here is what happens to me. The videos I land on picture and explain a toilet that's unlike mine or a floor that's totally different than mine. And the tools they recommend to do the job—you guessed it—I don't have them.

Trials always seem to bring us to some crossroad where inevitably we don't know what to do. Even when you know God allows those trials for a reason, and they are part of His plan, and even if you believe that in due time they will bring a great outcome, it is in the meantime that we struggle. Often it is not easy or plain to know which way to turn or which direction to go. The truth is we need wisdom to handle our trials. It is in gaining wisdom we can experience the kind of overflow that characterized the Macedonians (2 Cor. 8).

We are told not to give up so that we can finish well, lacking nothing (James 1:4). Now that phrase "lacking nothing" is the link to what he says next, for he knows that we do lack. Trials have a way of bringing out how far short we fall.

> "Our trials and suffering are not always the result of sin, but they almost always reveal sin."[13]

Sin stays around longer in my life if it is allowed to remain fuzzy and indistinct. It is amazing how trials stir my conscience and my sensitivity to the Spirit of God and the Word of God. I start to see the "cobwebs" in the corners of my heart. God has put the heat-lamp and the search light right where they need to be when my trial comes knocking.

One of His goals in my suffering is to wean me away from earthly idols and fleshly pursuits that destroy my stewardship of His blessings.

> "Before we go through pain and suffering, we are often so entranced by the world that we can barely hear his still, small voice. We treasure our blessedness in the meager terms of prosperity, physical health, success, family, friends and the like. God needs to wean us from earthly idols to cause us to focus entirely on him."[14]

Because our trials bring out so much that needs fixed in us, the need for wisdom becomes very obvious.

Why Wisdom Is Needed

The Lord knew that we would need great wisdom to endure all that our service to Christ would bring to us. We are engaging with some formidable foes like the world system, our own flesh, and of course our enemy-Satan. Our foes all have long standing experience in the battle. And wisdom is sorely needed if we would win the day.

Perhaps we need to define what we mean by wisdom. Simply put, wisdom is the ability to apply what we know to the problems of life. Jesus told the disciples that in times of trial they would be given a mouth and wisdom and also the ability to speak appropriately to the situation (Luke 21:15). Don't forget that biblical wisdom is also the ability to see the meaning and significance of things from God's perspective.

"For since, in the wisdom of God, the world did not know God through wisdom, it pleased God through the folly of what we preach to save those who believe" (1 Cor. 1:21).

It is one thing to know the Bible well. It is another thing to know:

[a] How to use the Bible correctly
[b] How to understand life and the world around us in light of that knowledge
[c] How to guide our conduct and that of others by the Bible

J. A. Motyer comments:

> "The wise person will be able to see life as James has pictured it; he will be able to make personal decisions and to shape life's pathway, so as to enjoy the progress towards maturity which God has promised. Such wisdom is a gift from God[15]

Question: If wisdom is a gift from God, then how do we get it? Answer: We ask for it! We ask God, who will not reproach us nor bawl us out, call us stupid, nor poke fun at our weakness and ignorance (James 1:5). God is approachable and kind and very gracious during our trials. He is a sympathetic high priest. Who can forget those comforting words in Hebrews 4:14–16?

"Since then we have a great high priest who has passed through the heavens, Jesus, the Son of God, let us hold fast our confession. For we do not have a high priest who is unable to sympathize with our weaknesses, but one who in every respect has been tempted as we are, yet without sin. Let us then with confidence draw near to the throne of grace, that we may receive mercy and find grace to help in time of need."

There is no doubt that we need grace. And we are promised this grace when we come to the throne of grace. Please know that this God of grace is generous. God does not set limits on his generosity. "To all," the text says. How beautiful! You don't have to deserve it to receive this wisdom. God is generous with it. It is not like God locks up the wisdom cabinet when He sees us coming even though we have not always acted wisely or biblically. God does not say, "You messed up. None for you today." Once we have God's wisdom, we can address the clay pot problems with hope. God in His wisdom knows that our clay pots will get cracks. That's where "crack fillers" come in.

> *God is approachable and kind and very gracious during our trials.*

Crack Fillers

As we limp along in our clay jar existence, we need to conclude our thoughts on clay pot living with some very practical "crack fillers."

Crack filler # 1: Don't let people blot out the reason for your hope—Christ Jesus.

Don't let other people blind you to His radiant presence and power in you. Our sympathetic high priest gives grace, mercy, and wisdom in abundant measure. Clay jar living is all about the treasure. Christ is our solid rock and anchor in the storms that trials produce.

Crack Filler # 2: Let the word of God hold you on mission and give you fresh heart. The distraction of our trials can gradually wean us away from complete reliance upon the Word of God. The result can be heavy discouragement and deep depression. The Word of God is the refresher of the wearied, burdened, and tried soul.

"The law of the Lord is perfect, reviving the soul..." (Ps. 19:7).

Remember that we live in a clay pot susceptible to cracks and holes. D. L. Moody used to say,

> "The only way to keep a broken vessel full is to keep it always under the tap."[16]

The Word of God is our water and our food (Jer. 15:16). It sustains us because trials can weaken us and make us dry and spiritually unhealthy. It keeps us from living at the edge of our margin where all the reserve is sucked away.

The Word of God is our light (Ps. 119:105). It guides us because trials have a way of bringing confusion and misdirection, increasing the darkness around us.

The Word of God is our wisdom (Deut. 4:6; Ps. 19:7; 119:98). It informs us with a reality that takes away the blinders that trials can impose.

The Word of God is our power (Heb. 4:12). It uplifts our spirit because trials tend to bury our emotions in a grave of hopelessness and despair (Ps. 19:8). Wield the sword of the Word of God with confidence in your trial because it is equal to all you are facing (Eph. 6:17).

Crack Filler # 3: Ramp up your prayer life. Asking for practical wisdom for what you endure in a trial is a sure crack filler for these old pots. Paul said the outer man was caving in. And he was so right. But the inner man can "keep on truckin'" because we have prayer as a resource for obtaining wisdom and help (2 Cor. 4:16; Heb. 4:16). And even when our prayers are not answered in the way we hoped or prayed, remember who decided how the prayers would be answered. It is the One who has declared an everlasting love for us.

Study Guide Questions

1. Think of a time when you prayed for God to give you something or spare you from something and God did not do it? What are ways we often handle that result? How could an unanswered prayer or a surprising answer to prayer (one you did not want or expect) affect your view of your trial?

2. How are you using the Word of God today to navigate whatever trial you are facing? Make a time chart of how often you return to the Word of God in a given week. Consistency is crucial. Keep a journal of what the Word of God is teaching you about trial management. What about memorizing a key passage that you can bring back to your mind regularly as a means of comfort and encouragement?

3. What is your gut reaction when someone brings up the notion that your trial is all part of God's plan? Do you resent that suggestion? Why or why not? How does your response define what you believe about God's wisdom and character?

4. Who do you think may be watching you very closely as you navigate your trial? What impressions will your children receive from your trial management? Will what they see help them build a good foundation for their own trials? What testimony do you raise to your neighbors and friends as they witness your journey through the jungle of testing? Will they see Christ more clearly or less clearly by your management of the trial?

5. How do you find yourself hogging the spotlight and centering everything on you during your trial? What is dangerous about this predetermined disposition to see only your own pain and trouble? How could this lead to a mismanagement of your trial and turn into a bad stewardship moment?

Chapter Two

Clay Pot Theology:
2 Corinthians 4

The problems we face in our clay pot living are very real. What makes clay pot living possible is the theological underpinnings given to us in the Word of God. We must learn to look at our clay jar lives in light of what God says in His Word about what is behind the bruises and cracks and struggles of clay jar living. If you don't know the what of your trials, then the why of your trials will always bother you. In this chapter we want to examine some basic theology behind our trial experiences. When we get traction from our theology, we will have the foundation to manage our trials well for God's glory.

There are two reasons we are given clay pot "container" lives. First, we live in these "containers" so that God may gain all the glory for what happens in and to the clay pot (1 Pet. 1:7).

> "The thing that God is most committed to is his own glory. But here's what you need to understand. His commitment to his own glory is your only hope."[17]

Second, these "containers" make us rely more on God and less on ourselves. (2 Cor. 1:8-10).

His commitment to his glory moves us to forsake our own glory and do the thing that we were created to do and that's to live for His glory. His use of such lowly containers forces us to rely solely on Him because the container itself has no glory or strength of its own. And that's the basis of a good, sound theology of stewardship in suffering. Let's take a closer look at this clay pot theology.

Good Theology in Trials

One of Charles Schulz's Peanuts cartoon strips shows Lucy looking at a deluge of rain and worrying about whether the whole world will flood. Linus reminds her that in the Bible God promised there would never be another world-wide flood. 'You've taken a great load off my mind,' Lucy says, to which Linus responds, 'Sound theology has a way of doing that!' What a reminder that managing our trials as good stewards of God must be based on sound theology.

Paul teaches, in 2 Corinthians, that we have an outer man and an inner man. The outer man is the clay pot covering, and the inner man is the new nature of God imparted to us at the moment of salvation (2 Cor. 5:17). How these two interact and what God has in store for both help us manage our trials with good theology.

The Theology of an Amazing Deposit

We begin with the amazing reality of Jesus Christ living in us, which Paul informs us is the hope of glory (Col 1:27). God made a deposit of His Son into our clay pot lives. God calls Jesus Christ a treasure in us. Our clay pots hold this treasure.

We need to take a closer look at the context of this treasure because this is what informs our theology. Paul says in 2 Corinthians 4:7–15:

"But we have this treasure in jars of clay, to show that the surpassing power belongs to God and not to us. We are afflicted in every way, but not crushed; perplexed, but not driven to despair; persecuted, but not forsaken; struck down, but not destroyed; always carrying in the body the death of Jesus, so that the life of Jesus may also be manifested in our bodies. For we who live are always being given over to death for Jesus' sake, so that the life of Jesus also may be manifested in our mortal flesh· So death is at work in us, but life in you. Since we have the same spirit of faith according to what has been written, "I believed, and so I spoke," we also believe, and so we also speak, knowing that He who raised the Lord Jesus will raise us also with Jesus and bring us with you into His presence. For it is all for your sake, so that as grace extends to more and more people it may increase thanksgiving, to the glory of God."

Clay pot living is all about what is in the pot not what is around the pot. This treasure is in us to show what Christ can do in a weak, flawed, and often cracked and damaged container.

The Theology of Weak Vessels and a Strong God

First of all, it should be very obvious to us that this treasure is *not* placed in a strong vessel (2 Cor. 4:7a mentions jars of clay), which suggests that the vessel is weak. Clay jars were the throwaway containers of the ancient world. They didn't last very long. They were used to store and transport water, olive oil, wine, grain, and even family treasures. They were also used for cooking, eating, drinking and storing leftovers. No one took note of clay jars any more than we would of fast-food containers today. You can see them littering the side of the road everywhere and it was much the same then with broken clay vessels.

R. Kent Hughes said,

> "They (the clay jars) were there for convenience. It was no great tragedy when such vessels were broken. They were cheap and easy to replace."[18]

So Paul describes us as clay jars. This illuminating treasure—Christ who is the light of the world—is resident in a clay jar. Are you thinking what I am thinking? Surely that cannot be the plan of God? Amazing. It is like putting your grandmother's diamond in a bag from McDonald's. That's what God did with us. I would never have done it that way. It seems like a gamble.

Recently, our car keys ended up in the garbage by mistake. I was throwing away the trash with my keys in my hand. After searching everywhere, I remembered back to the last time I saw them. I went to the garbage can and ripped aside bags and other debris and guess what? There were the keys, lying on the bottom of the trash can. You don't deliberately put valuable keys in the garbage. But it seems like that's what God did when He put Jesus in us.

Secondly, it should also be obvious to us that this treasure is not placed in a strong vessel for a *reason*. The text informs us of why God did this is. There is to be no mistake about where the power comes from:

"To show that the surpassing power belongs to God and not to us" (2 Cor. 4:7b).

In the midst of Paul's trial there was a moment when he even despaired of life itself. Paul thought he was going to die. All his strength was gone.

"For we do not want you to be ignorant, brothers, of the affliction we experienced in Asia. For we were so utterly burdened beyond our strength that we despaired of life itself. Indeed, we felt that we had received the sentence of death. But that was to make us rely not on ourselves but on God who raises the dead. He delivered us from such a deadly peril, and he will deliver us. On him we have set our hope that he will deliver us again" (2 Cor. 1:8–10).

We believers are only vessels in which God's power is exhibited. We are never powerful in ourselves. It's easy to misread what Paul says here. We can assume this is a way of gaining our power. We picture it like this: As we embrace our weakness God will pour his power into us so that we become powerful. The natural equation is: My weakness plus God's power equals my power."

> *We believers are only vessels in which God's power is exhibited. We are never powerful in ourselves.*

But that's not what Paul is saying at all. Rather, he teaches us that as we embrace our weakness, God fills us with His power so that His power is manifested through us. We do not become powerful. We remain weak. We do not grow in power. We grow in weakness. We go from weakness to weakness, so that we remain vessels of His power—ever weak and never strong in ourselves.

Kent Hughes relates this account in his commentary on 2 Corinthians about St. Francis:

> "Someone once asked St. Francis how he was able to accomplish so much. He replied, "This may be why: The Lord looked down from heaven and said, 'Where can I find the weakest, littlest man on earth?' Then he saw me and said, 'I've found him, and he won't be proud of it. He'll see that I am only using him because of his insignificance.'"[19]

So when God brings us through a trial it is so others can see His power in us and through us. They are puzzled about how we get through it at all. We don't get through it! That's the point. God's strength in us, however, does bring us through.

The take-away we gain is simply this: God must show us how weak we are in ourselves. Believers are only vessels in which God's power is exhibited.

Paul finally got this. He was a gifted and experienced servant of God who had been through a lot of different trials. You would think that all of these experiences would be sufficient for him to face these new difficulties and overcome them. But that's not so. Paul teaches us that he had to learn to embrace his weakness, so that God could fill him with His power. That's how God's power is manifested through us. Paul made this truth very clear for us in his confession in 2 Corinthians 12:7–10:

"So to keep me from becoming conceited because of the surpassing greatness of the revelations, a thorn was given me in the flesh, a messenger of Satan to harass me, to keep me from becoming conceited. Three times I pleaded with the Lord about this, that it should leave me. But He said to me, "My grace is sufficient for you, for my power is made perfect in weakness. Therefore I will boast all the more gladly of my weaknesses, so that the power of Christ may rest upon me. For the sake of Christ, then, I am content with weaknesses, insults, hardships, persecutions, and calamities. For when I am weak, then I am strong."

The word translated "rest" means "to spread a tent over." Paul considered his body to be like an earthly tent but the fact that Christ dwelt in his body meant that the glory of God had come into his body and made it a holy vessel. It also meant that the power of Christ was like a tent spread over his lowly, earthly tent-body to give him strength in his weakness.

The bottom line is this—and this bears repeating. We do not become powerful. We remain weak. We do not grow in power. We grow in weakness. And that's the context in which God demonstrates His power. That's the vehicle through which God manifests His glory. And this is where trial-management gets its start.

Cameron Cole, in his book *Therefore I Have Hope*, speaks about this matter:

> "When people try to tie up their pain and confusion in a tight little bow and, thereby, oversimplify the depth of their grief, they run the risk of creating distance from God and planting seeds of bitterness in their hearts. In this way, they try to 'be strong,' when the very response to which God calls them is to weakness."[20]

It's OK to be weak in His strength.

> "Paul learned that God permits trials, controls trials, and uses trials for His own glory. We can take heart that God is glorified through weak vessels."[21]

Third, Paul states another obvious point. This treasure makes the clay vessel strong in an unexpected way (2 Cor. 12:8–12). As an example of this great truth, Paul (all in the present tense by the way) tells us this was his own experience on more than one occasion.

Paul's confession is quite impressive. First he says that "we are afflicted in every way, but not crushed."

By all accounts, the pressure of his trials should have crushed the life out of him. The word *afflicted* literally means "pressure" and implies anything causing pain or distress like sorrow, loss, illness, or misfortune, etc.

Next, Paul confesses that "we are perplexed but not driven to despair." As problems and trials close in on him from all sides, Paul feels like his back is against the wall, not knowing which way to move. And yet it seems that Paul is never in a state of hopelessness. Phillip Hughes in his commentary on 2 Corinthians gives us some keen insight on this reality:

> "To be at the end of man's resources is not to be at the end of God's resources."[22]

Third, Paul is quick to confess that "we are persecuted, but not forsaken." The word *persecuted* here means "hunted." He knew the intense agony of being hunted and pursued like some animal quarry by his fellow men. Yet he knew he was not abandoned.

Finally, Paul admits that "we are struck down, but not destroyed..."

It might seem like we are knocked down never to get up again. But that's simply not true. This being knocked for a loop does not mean the end of you. When Paul was stoned by hostile Jews from Antioch and Iconium (who by the way followed him on to Lystra and eventually left him for dead) he was able to amazingly get up and go right back to ministry.

All ministry is costly not only in terms of what you give up to pursue it but also in the misunderstandings or abuse that can come from many directions.

All of these "but nots" show God's power working in the clay vessel. Human life is short, its form easily defaced and its fabric prone to destruction in a second. Paul talks about carrying around in his body the death of Jesus. This is his way of speaking of the physical and emotional pain associated with his ministry. It marks an earthen jar.

All ministry is costly not only in terms of what you give up to pursue it but also in the misunderstandings or abuse that can come from many directions. This principle of life arising out of death or costly sacrifice originates with Jesus. Hughes makes this case in the following words:

> "That the Christian does not succumb to his problems and difficulties is evidence that the life of Jesus is revealed within him...through the sovereign power of God."[23]

A Theology for the Sake of Others

In chapter one we discovered that our mission, in part, consists in serving others. We cannot forget that the treasure is in us for the sake of others (2 Cor. 4:13–15). Now this is proven by what we are able to say (4:13). And it is also proven by what we are able to know as well (4:14). For example, we serve people in our world who do not understand the matter of death. They are either ignorant of God's word on death or they are misinformed about the implications of what it means to die in a lost condition. If it is true that Christ has conquered death, the last enemy, then we can affirm that those who know Christ need not fear death or anything else for that matter. Did you ever notice that people try to figure out the meaning of death, yet the world has no answer to death? Until people are prepared to die, they are not really prepared to live. It seems to me, then, that our ultimate privilege in serving others is that it brings glory to God by offering the good news of Christ's death for sin. When a believer in the midst of his trial (which could even foreshadow his own death), exhibits calm confidence in Christ, then others can see what God is doing in us.

This is why Paul asked for prayer in the midst of his own affliction so that others would be led to give thanks to God.

"You also must help us by prayer, so that many will give thanks on our behalf for the blessing granted us through the prayers of many" (2 Cor. 1:11).

When others are affected by what they see God doing in us, God is glorified (4:15) and the Gospel is adorned (Titus 2:10). And that's just good stewardship.

> "Thus, when God so wills, the ministry of weak men
> can produce almighty effects: the blind see, the
> poor are humbled, and lofty cast down, and men's
> hearts changed, for God worketh with it." [24]

Aches and Pains Notwithstanding: The Theology of What's Coming

In the midst of trial, good management flows out of understanding where the ship is headed. First, Paul speaks about the incredible future of the believer. Our theology assures us God has prepared a good future for us.

"So we do not lose heart. Though our outer self is wasting away, our inner self is being renewed day by day. For this light momentary affliction is preparing for us an eternal weight of glory beyond all comparison, as we look not to the things that are seen but to the things that are unseen. For the things that are seen are transient, but the things that are unseen are eternal" (2 Cor. 4:16–18).

Some time ago the prime minister of Israel, Benjamin Netanyahu, addressed the US Congress. He spoke of Israel's past and future. He was articulate, candid and very forthright in explaining the dangers Israel faces today.

Those of us who read and believe the Bible know that God has a future for Israel. Yet today the future for Israel looks bleak in many ways.

The same can be said for our own lives at times. The present troubles, trials and struggles seem overwhelming and without end. But God bids us to look beyond today. There is another side to all of this.

Our physical bodies are called the outer man. When the outer man deteriorates, the inner man can grow (2 Cor. 4:16). Our outer man is under assault. Sorrows, troubles, needs, and sicknesses all assault our outer man. Those are the things Paul says are seen. How are we to handle those as a good steward of God?

Remember that the outer man belongs to this age and is in the process of passing away. That's what is happening to us. But we are not to be depressed or in despair about the outer man. The decaying of Paul's body was not meaningless. The pains, pressures, frustrations, afflictions and trials were not happening in vain. They were not going into some black hole of pointless struggle. Instead they were making something incredible for him far beyond anything he could compare it to.

No wonder Paul tells us that we are to gaze into our future. We are to listen to the promises and reassurances of God about where the bus is headed. The outer man, it is true, will be under assault and will waste away, but the inner man gets better and better. Because the inner man is connected to the eternal, it is being renewed day by day. It belongs to the age to come. The Lord is molding the real me into someone better, someone more like Jesus. He wants the old stuff to drop off and the new stuff to take its place. Bear in mind that Paul is not buying into the gnostic idea that the body is materially evil and that we should just ignore it. No, Paul is saying the best is yet to come for our physical bodies.

However, the renewal that he is talking about is not something we can see, feel, or experience right now. We accept this by faith. The things of this world seem so real because we can see them and feel them. That's why Paul says, in 2 Corinthians 4:18, that the things we see now will soon be gone. God is preparing a permanent, perfect home for us after our present bodies go down in death. He is going to raise our bodies from the dead. In other words, He is remaking us —that is what is happening in my life and that is how I manage trials. I am being repainted, the dents are getting hammered out, and the motor is headed for an overhaul

Peter Naylor commented in his book on 2 Corinthians about this very process:

> "Physical decay is pressed into service by God as a stepping stone towards the glory that will be."[25]

Paul uses this word *preparing* to mean to bring something into being. In this case it is pointing to the glory that's coming. The contrasts in the text are very stark here (2 Cor. 4:17–18):

"lightness and weight"
"present and eternal"
"trouble and glory"

Beyond all comparison literally reads "excessively excessive."

This verb *preparing* is in the present tense too, which is significant. The anticipation of what is to come—glory—intensifies as time goes on—day by day. So when you put all of this together, what Paul is saying here reads something like this:

"For the immediate lightness of our trouble produces for us in excess to excess an eternal glorious glory."

Naylor continues with this thought:

> "The writer does not suffer stoically with an uncomprehending endurance of what blind fate brings upon him, any more than he believes that his troubles enhance an imaginary credit account with God; the matter is far more subtle. Although Paul has been saved by the sufferings of Jesus alone, and rejoices that it is so, he is aware that his many sorrows usher him into a far better world, the two scenes bearing no comparison."[26]

Next, Paul speaks about the "marriage" of trial and glory. When the pressure comes on, the glory comes in (2 Cor. 4:17). The text here says affliction works for us. Literally, the verb here is *create*. Our light affliction is actually creating or producing for us an eternal weight of glory which is far beyond what we are presently experiencing. Our trial (affliction) "marries" us to a wonderful "mate" (glory). And that mate takes us into a glorious place. Sometimes it does not feel like we are headed for a glorious place because of the nature of our trials, but God says it is so.

There are ten basic words used for suffering in the Greek language and Paul uses five of them in this letter. The most frequently used word is *thlipsis*, which means, "a narrow, confined, under pressure" kind of thing. Here it is translated anguish (2 Cor. 2:4) and affliction (2 Cor. 1:4, 8 and 4:17). The pressure of our trials is very real. But that's not the end of the matter.

Think about this. God prepares us for our future tomorrow through the pressure of the trials He sends to us today.

God is preparing us for eternity. Using our troubles and trials, He prepares *for us* an eternal "weight of glory." This refers to an eternal house (see 2 Cor. 5:1ff) not built by any man. So at death we get a new body-house and a new world to live in which is absolutely spectacular. It is so heavy in weight and value that everything pressing us today and trying us now is lightweight in comparison (2 Cor. 4:17). The glory is coming. Hang on!

God is also preparing us for a new life. Since we are not quite ready spiritually or emotionally for this radical change, God has to prepare us for the new life we are going to receive (2 Cor. 5:5). In other words, God prepares the future for us and us for the future— both objective and subjective preparations.

God is preparing us to be patient and wait on Him. Now it is at this point I find my greatest struggle. I want the trials and their lessons to quickly come to an end, so I can get on to the good stuff. David Powlison, in his book *God's Grace in Your Suffering*, is quick to point out this struggle:

> "We want problems to have quick solutions so we can move on to something else. But God has made our souls to work on agricultural time and child-rearing time....The problems of suffering don't have quick 'solutions.'"[27]

A Theological Reality: Does God Ever Rescue Us from Trials?

So if I have to stay in the trial for a while, does that mean that God is not going to rescue me from it? Is my theology a "microwave" belief, where I put my trial in and—zap—two minutes later the trial is over?

One theological mistake we make is pinning our hopes on being quickly rescued from our trials as if God is bound to do that. Our hope must not be in the changing of the circumstances we are in, but in the God who is over the circumstances we are in.

2 Corinthians 1:10 reminds us that God often does rescue us from our trials. "He delivered us from such a deadly peril, and he will deliver us. On him we have set our hope that he will deliver us again." However, God does not always rescue us immediately nor does God rescue us in the way we hope. Warren Wiersbe put it this way in the Transformation Bible:

God does not always rescue us immediately nor does God rescue us in the way we hope.

> "Sometimes God rescues us from our trials, and at other times he rescues us in our trials."[28]

Romans 5:3–5 speaks of this kind of rescue:

"More than that, we rejoice in our sufferings, knowing that suffering produces endurance, and endurance produces character, and character produces hope, and hope does not put us to shame, because God's love has been poured into our hearts through the Holy Spirit who has been given to us."

The progression Paul speaks of in this text is important for us to understand if we are going to appreciate what God is up to in our trials as a way of preparing us for the future. If we believe that God is at work in them, then we will have a totally different perspective of what rescue means.

There are many ways to face suffering and trials. Most people complain about trials. Some people endure them bravely. This enduring is sometimes called being stoical. The Stoics were a group of Greek and Roman philosophers who refused to be affected either by joy or by sorrow. But believers in Christ can actually rejoice in suffering. How can that be? Paul tells us that rejoicing in our sufferings is possible because of what we know about rescue.

Here is what we know about God rescuing us in our trials (and it is what we know that gives us reasons to rejoice).

First, we know that suffering produces endurance (Rom. 5:3). The word *endurance* means that in spite of sufferings we can go on without despairing. We will not go under. We will make it through. Here again we are assured that endurance (being able to make it through) will be ours. Endurance is a form of rescue.

Secondly, we know that endurance produces character (Rom. 5:4). This word here has the idea of testing something to see whether it is true or genuine. If it passes the test, it is proven or approved. Literally, the word means "approved-ness." The same idea is found in James 1:3, 12 and in 1 Peter 1:17. It's God's way of showing the world that trusting Him, believing in Him is the real deal. Character is a form of rescue.

Third, we know that character produces hope (Rom. 5:4). Hope is simply faith about the future. As the result of our trials and sufferings we get more confidence about the future. Having passed the test, we can be confident of coming successfully through future trials and tests. Hope then is a form of rescue.

Fourth, we know that this hope will not put us to shame (Rom. 5:5). Hope is confidence in something that's certain. Hope does not leave us shamed, embarrassed, disappointed or disillusioned in the end because we followed and trusted the Lord in our trials. Why doesn't it? Scripture tells us it is because God's love has been poured into our hearts through the Holy Spirit who has been given to us. What a rescue!

Lastly, we know that God's love has been poured into our hearts (Rom. 5:5).

This is the basis of everything which we receive from God. We can see God's love for us by the gift of His Son on the cross and by the gift of His Spirit to us. The assurance of God's love is a form of rescue.

In light of these rescues from trial that we enjoy, we can say with Paul:

"For I consider that the sufferings of this present time are not worth comparing with the glory that is to be revealed to us" (Rom. 8:18).

Paul was tasting the effects of God's ongoing rescue of him in his trials. His hope was very real! You see what we possess now (God's grace) is the basis of our hope for tomorrow of receiving more (God's glory).

Think of it like this. A child who knows that his father loves him now, is, for that reason, sure that his father will help him in the future. That's why we can trust God for the future. And that's the basis of our hope. All this work being done in our lives is being done by God Himself, through His Spirit. It is as if God has us like an athlete going through steps of training so that we are prepared for glory and the glory is prepared for us. Somewhere in my reading I came across this little gem:

> *A child who knows that his father loves him now, is, for that reason, sure that his father will help him in the future.*

"There is nothing accidental in the life of an obedient child of God (Psalm 31:15 my times are in your hands). All born-again believers are in training for rulership."[29]

The Theology of the Temporary Vs. the Theology of the Permanent

Training in trials, like training in athletic competitions can be arduous and wearying. One forgotten factor we often push aside in our trials has to do with their nature. They are *all* temporary. All of them. Temporary *is* temporary. Trials are not designed by God to last forever.

Dr. Harry Ironside, the famous pastor of Moody Church used to say,

"When I was upset by troubles, I go to the Bible, and I never get far before I read 'It came to pass.' And I say 'Bless the Lord it didn't come to stay—it came to pass!'"[30]

There is a coming out place. David experienced this very thing:

"He sent from on high, he took me; he drew me out of many waters. He rescued me from my strong enemy and from those who hated me, for they were too mighty for me. They confronted me in the day of my calamity, but the LORD was my support. He brought me out into a broad place; he rescued me, because he delighted in me" (Ps. 18:16–19).

What sweet words. "He brought me out."

Knowing something will not last and will not have its teeth in us forever helps us to endure through God's strength because it paints an entirely different picture of time versus eternity. It's like when you finish a grueling sports practice, you know it is over and game day is coming.

So here is a little principle to tuck away. When the temporary (seen) gets you down, the eternal (unseen) will lift you up (2 Cor. 4:18).

Warren Wiersbe perhaps sums this up best:

> "We value the material because it can be used to promote the spiritual, and not for what it is in itself."[31]

The material "thing" that's happening to us is not where the value is. It is what that material thing will bring in spiritual value that matters. And that material thing—the trial that's happening to us—is temporary.

Don't lose sight of the fact that the temporary must be seen as temporary. Don't assign permanent status to any suffering happening to us here. It has a label on it: "Temporary." That helps us manage those trials as good stewards. It won't last. It is not here to stay. It can't move in and take over. It's nature is temporary.

This is what Peter meant when he tells us in 1 Peter 1:5–7:

"Who by God's power are being guarded through faith for a salvation ready to be revealed in the last time. In this you rejoice, though now for a little while, if necessary, you have been grieved by various trials, so that the tested genuineness of your faith—more precious than gold that perishes though it is tested by fire—may be found to result in praise and glory and honor at the revelation of Jesus Christ."

Let's look a little more carefully at the great contrast between what is temporary and what is eternal (permanent). That "little while" says my trial is not a permanent houseguest. Someday it will be gone.

Peter Randolph, a slave in the mid-1800s, chronicled in his autobiography how underground worship services were an outlet for their hope of glory. He wrote that slaves would wander off plantations to assemble in a secure location. They would sing, pray, preach and derive encouragement from such times.

> "As they closed the meeting, they would sing one more hymn reminding each other of the joys of heaven that awaited them and exclaim: 'Thank God, I shall not live here always.'"[32]

These dear slaves allowed the eternal to dominate the temporary. They confessed that they would not live in their trials always. They were looking ahead.

Consider the word *look*, in 2 Corinthians 4:18, which has the force of meaning "to fix your gaze on, to concentrate your attention on." When Paul was hurting, he fixed his eyes not on how heavy the hurt was now , but on how heavy the glory will be that's coming. The eternal must be seen as permanent and it brings glory that will not go away. When the eternal comes, there is no going back to the way things are here. Hallelujah and *amen*. (There needs to be a good amen here.)

Eternal *is* permanent. The eternal lasts, it is written in permanent marker—rock solid, no change, here-to-stay kind of thing. Just because the eternal is not seen does not mean it is no less real. You see what is happening to you today. You feel it, you hurt because of it. But the tomorrow that's coming is just as real and we don't see it yet, we don't feel it yet, we have not experienced it yet, but it is as real as the stuff we are experiencing today.

That's Paul's point here. Fix your gaze ahead. The most precious and important realities in the world are beyond our physical senses.

There is a comparison in the text that helps us see all that Paul is telling us here and it looks like this:

2 Cor. 4:17	2 Cor. 4:18	2 Cor. 5:1
temporary light suffering	things that are seen	our earthly tent house
an eternal weight of glory	things that are not seen	a house/ building from God

The Reality of Tent Theology

The earthly tent is coming down. Paul is convinced that when the tent comes down here (as it will), the building goes up there.

"For we know that if the tent that is our earthly home is destroyed, we have a building from God, a house not made with hands, eternal in the heavens. For in this tent we groan, longing to put on our heavenly dwelling, if indeed by putting it on we may not be found naked. For while we are still in this tent, we groan, being burdened—not that we would be unclothed, but that we would be further clothed, so that what is mortal may be swallowed up by life. He who has prepared us for this very thing is God, who has given us the Spirit as a guarantee" (2 Cor. 5:1–9).

Several years ago, Sue and I drove by the Hearst Castle, near San Luis Obispo on the coast of California. It is quite an impressive structure. This castle, with its magnificent building and its beautiful grounds, has behind it the story of the Hearst family. When Mr. Hearst was alive and invited guests to his home, the guests were given one rule. They were absolutely forbidden to break this rule upon pain of immediate exclusion from the castle. To do so meant that they were never again allowed entrance to the grounds. That rule was that no one should, in Mr. Hearst's presence, utter the word *death*. He tried to ignore death, to exclude it from his thinking. But, as always happens to men like that, death caught up with him one day. He himself died, and the castle passed into the hands of the state. All that was once his is no longer even in the possession of his family. His future was one of dim uncertainty.

It is not so with us. Our trials are but preparing us for the next great chapter in our lives and that's what we are considering. We are not afraid to mention death knowing that it is not the end for us who know Jesus. Paul's discovery about his future gave him strength to manage his trials even in light of death itself.

The Theology of What We Know

The word *know* is a wonderful word, and in the context of a believer's future hope, it is a word that makes certain facts clear about life beyond death.

Knowing speaks of what we can be certain of. We read in 2 Corinthians 5:1, "For we know...."

It is striking, is it not? "We know," says the Apostle Paul. There is nothing uncertain about it at all. As Christians we are certain of a number of things that our nonbelieving friends cannot know.

Here is what we are certain of.

First, we are certain we live in a tent house. Twice he calls the present body "a tent." He sees it as only a temporary dwelling place. We spoke about our tent-bodies earlier. These are structures that were never meant to be permanent dwellings.

Our family used to go camping and started out doing so in a tent. A couple of days are fun. A couple of weeks? Not so much. Truth be known we were glad to get out of the tent. You feel the weather more in a tent. Hot, cold, wet, wind—you know the drill (apologies to avid tent campers).

Second, we are certain that this tent-house is falling apart. In this tent there is a lot of groaning going on. Do you ever listen to yourself when you get up in the morning? You don't look so good and you certainly don't sound so good. Some people are not fit to live with until they get that first cup of coffee. I don't know what it is about coffee, but it does seem to purge some groans out of us. It is pretty evident that the apostle is right, isn't it? Yes, we do groan.

The truth is we are falling apart—every day. There is the groan of our present experience (2 Cor. 5:4a). The tent is beginning to sag. The stakes are loosening, and the pegs are growing wobbly. We discover that things are not going along as they once were. Every now and then, especially after we have been exercising strenuously, we find these words to be literally true—we groan. If we are not battling a toothache, we are struggling with a headache and on it goes. The groans keep coming.

I came across an illustration from one of Ray Stedman's sermons a while ago on the internet (you can find anything there, right?) entitled "It's Later Than You Think."

"Everything is farther than it used to be. It's twice as far from my house to the station now, and they've added a hill which I've just noticed. The trains leave sooner, too, but I've given up running for them because they go faster than they used to. Seems to me they're making staircases steeper than in the old days. And have you noticed the small print they're using lately? Newspapers are getting farther and farther away when I hold them. I have to squint to make out the news. Now it's ridiculous to suggest that a person my age needs glasses, but it's the only way I can find out what's going on without someone reading aloud to me. And that isn't much help because everybody seems to speak in such a low voice I can scarcely hear them."[33]

Another man put it this way:

Times are changing. The material in my clothes, I notice, shrinks in certain places. Shoelaces are so short they're next to impossible to reach. And even the weather is changing. It's getting colder in winter and the summers are much hotter than they used to be. People are changing, too. For one thing, they're younger than they used to be when I was their age. On the other hand, people my own age are so much older than I am.

I ran into an old friend the other night, and he had changed so much he didn't recognize me. "You've put on weight, Bob," I said.

"It's this modern food," he said. "It seems to be more fattening."

I got to thinking about poor Bob this morning while I was shaving. Stopping for a moment, I looked at my own reflection in the mirror. You know, they don't use the same kind of glass in mirrors, anymore.[34]

But groans are not all that's happening in this tent house. Along with the groans, there are the sighs. We long for something better. We could call this the sigh of future expectancy (2 Cor. 5:4b). We know that life is only temporary. We sense that there is coming a time when this earthly tent will be destroyed. We all face it, don't we? Despite the advances that have been made in medical science and the remarkable things that technology has done, it is still true that the death rate remains exactly what it has been for centuries: a flat 100 percent.

This earthly tent must be destroyed. But the apostle says, "We know that we have a house waiting for us, eternal in the heavens." An eternal house is waiting. It is for this we sigh. Notice how Paul explains our future house.

Paul speaks of us having a building. He is referring to a body (2 Cor. 5:1). If he could describe our present body as a tent, then is it not fitting that he should describe the resurrection body as a house? After all, a tent is temporary; a house is permanent. We will move from the temporary to the permanent, from the tent to the house eternal in the heavens.

But we face a problem. The tent coming down—whether it is our tent or the tent of someone we love—is a very heart-wrenching experience. The finality of the tent no longer being here is very painful. God is so honest with us. He speaks of the groaning and sighing that goes on as long as we are in this tent. The believer who is released from this tent knows groaning and sighing no longer, but we who are still in the tent-house must contend with such experiences.

Our Theology Declares That Good Changes Are Coming

The fear of all connection with the present life being lost at death is untrue. Paul says we go on living in a body made for there like our bodies are made for here.

What we must know is that God clothes us in a temporary body until the day of resurrection. How do we know that? All the scenes in heaven that John saw in Revelation reveal the saints clothed in white robes, and singing praises and interacting together. He could see them in their physical forms.

Not only that, but remember Jesus and the three disciples on the Mount of Transfiguration saw Moses and Elijah appearing in some bodily form, yet they had not yet been resurrected nor given their permanent resurrection bodies. There they were talking, communicating, and being recognized for who they were on earth.

Now we don't know what kind of bodies these are. But here is what we do know for sure. When the tent comes down, believers go directly into the presence of Christ at death (2 Cor. 5:8). They are conscious and in command of all of their faculties. (Remember Lazarus and the rich man in Luke 16?) Their personalities continue.

They will be the same people they were on earth, though believers will be perfected and sanctified. It appears that our genders will be retained as well. Some people falsely believe we earn our wings and become angels. That's not taught anywhere in the Bible.

When the tent comes down, personal knowledge continues in the eternal state (the rich man in hell knew he had five brothers). Remember your family reunions? Do you think you will know less in heaven than you do here? Did you ever notice that the three disciples on the Mount of Transfiguration knew Moses and Elijah but had never met them before? I don't think they had name tags. In heaven we will have far more knowledge than we have here.

When the tent comes down personal love continues in eternity. Remember that the rich man was concerned about his family lest they come to that place?

And when the tent comes down personal feelings continue. Remember in Revelation 6:9–10, where the martyred saints cried out to the Lord to avenge them? Our struggle with sin will be over, but we will be aware of who we really are. There will be no doubt in our minds that we have just moved from one place to another without an intermediate stop.

Think of Israel in the wilderness. They lived a camp-style life until they entered the land of promise where there were houses and permanent places to live in.

In John 1:14 this tent metaphor was used of the Lord Jesus coming in the flesh—literally. "The Word became flesh and pitched His tent among us."

So this tent-house could be referring to a temporary body until our resurrected and glorified body is ready. The emphasis is on the reality of a permanent structure with foundations as compared to our temporary tent-abode here.

"Not made with hands," means not originating here on this earth. It is not attached to the temporariness of here, but the permanence of there.

The Theology of Managing the Resurrected Body

One of the things we are learning down here, in this body, is how to manage the resurrection body. That will be a body fully subjected to the spirit. How many times have you said when someone invites you to do something, "Well, the spirit is willing, but the flesh is weak." You mean, "I wish I could; I'd love to do it, as far as my desire is concerned, but I find my body unable to respond—the flesh is weak."

But in the resurrection body this will not be true; there the body will be equal to the demands of the spirit. Anything we want to do, we will find we are able to do. What a glorious experience that will be.

That's why Paul says, in 2 Corinthians 5:4, that he longs to be further clothed (not unclothed—he does not have a death wish).

More about the Theology of Trial and Reward

Not only do our bodies change, but our ship finally comes in. Paul reminds us that when the paycheck is thin here, the payoff is huge there.

"So whether we are at home or away, we make it our aim to please him. For we must all appear before the judgment seat of Christ, so that each one may receive what is due for what he has done in the body, whether good or evil" (2 Cor. 5:9–10).

God does not guarantee that all our rewards come to us now. When we think of the thin paycheck here, we must think of the day we will be rewarded for our faithful service (2 Cor. 5:9–10). After all, not all we do here issues in what we would count as successful.

A lot of people around us live for money and possessions, amassing as much as they can, while others are busy investing their time in education or entertainment, hoping to find long-lasting value and enjoyment. But the believer's payday has not yet arrived. Though God does bring blessing and fruit to us in this life, it does not all come to us today.

Imagine that you are a stock trader at your office, researching the best stocks to invest. You feel a nudge on your shoulder and look up to see Jesus Christ himself standing beside your desk. He smiles, reaches into his pocket and gives you a sheet with the ten best companies to invest your money in for the next fifty years. You can't believe what just happened. God has given you the winners you were trying to predict. You are astonished at the grace of God and are excited to go "all in" with your money into those companies. Anything less than going "all in" would be the waste of a lifetime.[35]

The truth is, if you are a Christian, God has already given you the incredible opportunity of knowing the future so that you may be able to invest your life wisely in the light of it. The Scriptures tell us specifically about the rewards Christ has in store for his own. (Matthew 5:12; 1 Corinthians 3:8; Philippians 3:14; 2 Timothy 4:8; 1 Peter 5:4).

The Theology of Encouragement

In view of the certainty of this coming payoff, Paul says twice that our present life should be marked with courage. "We are of good courage." This means more than merely a stiff upper lip. It means, rather, that we should be full of encouragement, joy, and expectation about what is coming.

Paul gives two reasons we have for embracing encouragement:

First, we can be encouraged because we have the Holy Spirit as a guarantee (2 Cor.1:22; Eph. 1:14). God is preparing us for this great life ahead. He is getting us ready. He is teaching us how to walk by faith, and not by sight. To encourage our spirits during this present time, he has given us the Holy Spirit as a guarantee that the resurrection will happen.

How does the presence of the Holy Spirit in our hearts serve as a guarantee? Well, think about the Holy Spirit's past experience along this line. In 2 Corinthians 4:14, Paul says, "Knowing that he who raised the Lord Jesus will raise us also...."

The Holy Spirit has already done this once. He knows how to do it, for He raised the Lord Jesus. So we have a guarantee that He can perform this feat with us too (Rom. 8:11).

Think too of his present ministry in our daily lives.

"So we do not lose heart." (That's the same idea as "we are of good courage.") Though our outer nature is wasting away, our inner nature is being renewed every day" (2 Cor. 4:16).

Our spirits are being renewed and refreshed by the Spirit of God (Eph. 4:23).

The Spirit has not only effected a resurrection with the body, as in the case of Jesus, but he has been doing it with our spirits every day since we became Christians: renewing us, refreshing us, resurrecting us so we do not get discouraged or downcast in spirit. He knows how to stir us to fresh life, and to renew us daily as we rest upon the power of the indwelling life of God.

The presence of God in our lives is a remarkable deterrent to discouragement. The Navy SEALS had a phrase that they used during the "Vietnam era: "Always keep one foot in water." No matter what enemy they're facing, SEALs are confident that if they get into water, they will have the advantage, because they are trained to thrive in that environment, which is dangerous and even fatal to everyone else. Pastor Banning Liebscher reminds us that:

"The presence of God is to us as believers like water to a Navy SEAL. For us, the presence of God is where we thrive, and where the lies of the enemy die. We're called to "always keep one foot" in the presence of God, because the moment we retreat to His presence, the lies of discouragement, hopelessness, powerlessness fall away, and we are filled with the truth that He is with us, that there is boundless hope for our situation, and that we are not alone."[36]

Secondly, we can be encouraged because someday we will head home. Notice the words of this text:

"We know that while we are at home in the body we are away from God" (2 Cor. 5:6).

But the text goes on to say, "We would rather be away from the body and at home with the Lord" (2 Cor. 5:8).

Did you catch that? We Christians keep talking about "going home to be with the Lord," but have you noticed that you are already at home when you are in the body? In other words, you will never get away from home. We are at home right now in the body. We feel at ease, we feel relaxed about being in a physical body. We like this physical life, it is comfortable. We do not particularly want to leave it to be disembodied. But when we do, we will find that we will be just as much at home there as we were in the body down here. It is still home. It will be no different in that respect.

> *One thing must always be characteristic of us, namely, that we make it our aim to please Him.*

The Theology of God's Pleasure

There is another eternal issue that should preoccupy us and that has to do with the pleasure of God.

"So whether we are at home or away, we make it our aim to please Him" (2 Cor. 5:9).

Whether we are down here or up there, it makes no difference. One thing must always be characteristic of us, namely, that we make it our aim to please Him.

"For we must all appear before the judgment seat of Christ, so that each one may receive what is due for what he has done in the body, whether good or evil" (2 Cor. 5:10).

Once again we are dealing with a stewardship issue. Paul views the management of our lives, even in the face of trials, as a stewardship matter before the judgment seat of Christ. And pleasing God in that management should be one of our greatest concerns. We have already learned that on that day we will receive our full paycheck of reward for serving Christ.

We are going to receive what is due for what we have done in the body, whether good or evil. Now the mention of evil doing for the believer is somewhat puzzling.

The Theology of Good and Evil

The question that comes to us after reading this verse is this: What constitutes good or evil? It is made clear in the context of 2 Corinthians 5:9 that good is what pleases God. Evil is what displeases God. Our aim must be to please Him, for what pleases Him is good. When we stand at the judgment seat of Christ and all our life is evaluated, we will see that only what is done for Christ's pleasure can be called good. In the midst of trial, I can do evil. I can displease God and that very decision can spoil my stewardship of what God brought into my life for my good and His glory.

What is the issue that marks a thing as either good or evil? What essential ingredient must there be to please God? Hebrews 11:6a answers this question: "Without faith it is impossible to please Him."

Faith is the response of an obedient heart to God's word. It is acting according to what God says. Without that it is impossible to please Him.

Faith is acting on the basis of the written word and in dependence on the indwelling power of the Living Word, the Lord Jesus Christ. Without that element of faith, motivating and undergirding each activity of life, the most sincere action or attitude is unacceptable to God (Heb. 11:6), and constitutes evil.

One of these days we who know Jesus will stand before the judgment seat of Christ who, not in anger but in truth, will examine our lives (2 Cor. 5:10). No matter how much praise we have received here on this earth from others for the way we have acted, the only thing that will count on that day is what He says about us. All that will be of value will be what we have done in response to His Word, and in obedience to what He has commanded. Thus, we will have lived by faith and not by sight. The Day of Judgment for us is also a day of reward. What we suffered here will be more than compensated for over there.

> *Faith is acting on the basis of the written word and in dependence on the indwelling power of the Living Word, the Lord Jesus Christ.*

Clay-Pot Theology Summarized

As we close this chapter, think about what managing your trials as a good steward means from the perspective of a clay pot. In the eyes of the world of Paul's day, Paul was a failure. He suffered, he lost ground in ministry, he witnessed the departure of close friends.

Read 2 Corinthians 11, and look at all the lonely, hurting, disappointing experiences he had. Yet Paul is not taken down by any of it. He manages his trials as a good steward and even testified to that fact in his last letter: "I have fought the good fight, I have finished the race, I have kept the faith" (2 Tim. 4:7).

That's a pretty good summary of the ideal steward—the goal toward which all of us must aim.

Let's rehearse how we are to manage our trials theologically in these clay pots.

1: You have an outer man and an inner man. Don't let your outer man dominate your inner man. When the outer man deteriorates, the inner man can keep growing. Keep feeding that inner man on God's word.

2: Never allow the temporary to overshadow the permanent. When the temporary gets us down, the eternal picks us up. Be a good Scotsman and go for that which lasts.

3: Never let the thin paychecks of today blot out the coming reward of tomorrow. When the pressure comes on, the glory comes in. Glory follows the faithful at the end of their trials.

> "Everything that is now semiconscious, tainted, and half-baked will then be clear-minded, holy, and utterly fulfilled."[37]

There is a payoff coming beyond anything we can imagine.

Maybe today God is calling you to re-manage your trials in light of what is real about today and tomorrow. Go to prayer confessing that your sight has only been filled with the temporary, and that you have forgotten to look through the lens of God's promises to the real stuff that's yet to come. Our theology is sound.

Or perhaps you need to come to Christ to save you. All you have without Christ is the reality of this world and the awful reality of the next world. There is a future which has no glory for you, but only immense suffering and eternal heartache separated from God forever. To know Christ as your Savior changes all of that. That's why Paul said that anyone who is in Christ is a new creation (2 Cor. 5:17). When you repent of your sins and place your faith in Christ alone to save you, you will have passed from death into life and the future is settled (Mark 1:15; John 3:36; 5:24). And that is *good* theology.

Study Guide Questions

1. Paul says that God's work of grace toward him was not in vain. (1 Cor. 15:10: "But by the grace of God I am what I am, and His grace toward me was not in vain. On the contrary, I worked harder than any of them, though it was not I, but the grace of God that is with me."). Can we testify to this in our own experience?

    He goes on to say that it inspired him to work harder than others and then confesses that it was in reality the grace of God at work in his life. How is God's grace at work in your life? Where do you see evidences of God's grace toward you even in your trials? Does this energize you as it did Paul? Why or why not?

2. Should the presence of Christ as a treasure in us affect how we manage our clay-jar experiences? If so, in what way? Think about this: Is the jar an end in itself? If it is not, then what is the end God has in view in light of our treasure?

3. What are some reactions we display when our trial lasts longer than we think it should? What is it about the duration of a time of suffering that sucks away our hope and lands us in the area of depression?

4. How does the future of my jar-life help me face the trials I must weather in this clay jar today? When you know something good is coming, does your perspective change? In what way?

5. How important is good theology to my understanding of trial management?

Chapter Three

Living in the Overflow
Text: 2 Corinthians 8

No Easy Fix

Many of us can recall when Starbucks announced their new campaign slogan "Race Together" to get people talking about race issues. Solving human problems is not easy at all. Putting words on a cup to promote change in the human heart does not work. And we should not be surprised that Starbucks pulled the campaign after only a few days.

Sorrows and troubles defy easy solutions from our paltry human resources. Nothing seems to fit or work for very long.

It is that way when we are wrestling with trials too. Sorrows and troubles defy easy solutions from our paltry human resources. Nothing seems to fit or work for very long.

Take faith, for instance, when we are wrestling with trials. I am going to say it and bring it out on the table. Faith is not natural for you and I. Paul David Tripp observes, in his *New Morning Mercies* devotional, how true this statement is of us.

> "Doubt is natural. Fear is natural. Living on the basis of your experience is natural. Pushing the current catalog of personal "what-ifs" through your mind before you go to sleep or when you wake up in the morning is natural. Envying the life of someone else and wondering why it isn't your life is natural. Wishing that you were more sovereign over people, situations and locations is natural. Manipulating your way into personal control so you can guarantee that you will get what you think you need is natural. Looking horizontally for the peace that you will only ever find vertically is natural. Giving way to despondency, discouragement, depression or despair is natural. Numbing yourself with busyness, material things, media, food, or some other substance is natural."[38]

No, faith is simply not natural to us. So in grace God grants us the strength to believe. Paul David Tripp goes on to observe that

> "There is no more counterintuitive function to the average, sin-damaged human being than faith in God."[39]

As human beings we often put faith in a lot of things, but not in a God we cannot see, or hear, or a God who makes promises so grand they seem impossible to keep.

So the next time we face the unexpected, or a moment of sorrow or great difficulty we really don't want to go through, remember that such a moment doesn't picture a God who has forgotten you, but one who is near to you and doing in you a very good thing. Tripp adds one more thought to God's way of addressing our faith-in-trial issue:

> "God rescues us from thinking that we can live the life we were meant to live while relying on the inadequate resources of our own wisdom, experience, righteousness, and strength. And He is transforming you into a person who lives a life shaped by radical God-centered faith....He will not take us off his wheel until His fingers have molded us into those who really do believe and do not doubt."[40]

That's why if we are ever going to manage these trials as stewards of God we have to go to the word of God for our directions and help

"Faith comes by hearing and hearing by the Word of God" (Rom. 10:17).

But here is the problem I have. How do you pull off this faith living thing in the everyday mess we call life, especially when trials can be so preoccupying and draining to my faith? Can anyone really do that?

There is a group of people that learned how to do that. They learned to live in what I like to call the overflow of grace. We are going to examine carefully these folk who were in the middle of some serious trial...yet they were managing their trials as good stewards in light of God's grace to them. Their theology was working. Their faith was alive. And grace was the reason.

Macedonians—Happy Folk, Poor Folk

The Macedonian believers were not building their lives on proud achievements and material conquests (see James 4:6). Macedonia was a beautiful tract of land in the middle of the plains of the Gulf of Thessalonica. Their land was situated in the great river valleys of the Balkan Mountains. It became known for its timber and precious metals. The churches in this region were planted by the Apostle Paul on his second missionary journey (Philippi, Thessalonica, Berea, etc.). They were called the "Barbarian North" by other regions close to them. Yet the group of believers in this area acted nothing like their counterparts. They were not a proud, domineering, and filled with "fleshly competition" kind of people, as was characteristic of people from this region. Though the believers in this area lived in such a prosperous place, and no doubt were used to having a lot of material wealth, when persecution came to them and they lost most of what men count as vital to the good life, they continued to thrive. Christ had done a transforming work of grace in them. From a proud, materialistically preoccupied society, these believers lived with the setbacks persecution brought to them with humble grace and radiant faith.

> *God's grace accompanies all of our trials and that is what makes it possible to give, to serve, to love, and to go on under the severest of afflictions.*

You can't miss seeing an attractive humility about the way they handled their trials. And the explanation is very simple: They learned to live in the overflow of grace. God's grace produced some very deep marks upon them in the midst of their suffering.

Mark # 1: God's gift of grace sustained them and strengthened them in the midst of deep trial.

God gave his undeserved favor to them as a gift.

Paul mentions the word *grace* in this section several times as a significant key to what was happening with the Macedonians (2 Cor. 8:1, 4, 6–7). God's grace accompanies all of our trials and that is what makes it possible to give, to serve, to love, and to go on under the severest of afflictions. It is not that we have grace in ourselves but that we have grace given to us by the power and presence of the Holy Spirit. Grace is the only explanation for what these people did.

Notice that God's grace came to them against the backdrop of a severe test of affliction. They were being persecuted and suffered much loss (extreme poverty) because of their testimony. Yet you do not find them hunkering down and saying, "Well we are so strapped we cannot do anything for anyone else. We have to take care of ourselves." That's often how we think. But they had been touched by the grace of God. Paul says that their severe test of affliction and their extreme poverty, instead of being a cause for not serving sacrificially, actually became an additional cause for their sacrifice. We will look later at their unexpected generosity. But don't miss this underlying truth. Their generous response was an overflow of grace working in them, so much so that their sacrificial offering was called "this act of grace" (2 Cor. 8:6–7). When God's grace is at work in you, grace flows out of you even in severe trial. This overflow of grace marks us as people related to Jesus Christ because a couple of verses later in this passage we read: "For you know the grace of our Lord Jesus Christ, that though he was rich, yet for your sake he became poor, so that you by his poverty might become rich" (2 Cor. 8:9). We live in the overflow of such grace. In their severe affliction, the Macedonians experienced an overflow of grace which enabled them to do what would have been unthinkable without grace. And those acts of sacrificial service were done in the midst of severe affliction. Managing our trials as a good steward is not possible without the grace of God. And He freely gives it to us.

Mark # 2: God's grace made them just plain joyful folk in spite of their affliction

Because of God's grace they also experienced an overflow of joy even though they had trouble.

"We want you to know, brothers, about the grace of God that has been given among the churches of Macedonia, for in a severe test of affliction, their abundance of joy and their extreme poverty have overflowed in a wealth of generosity on their part" (2 Cor. 8:1–2).

Joy is unexpected here especially when it is connected with affliction. Paul wanted his audience in Corinth to know about the grace of God given among the churches in Macedonia. It was in a severe test of affliction (lit. great testing arising from trouble) that they gave of themselves and their resources joyfully. Here is what was going on.

Paul had a plan to take some offerings to the believers in Jerusalem who were suffering great lack because of their loyalty to Christ. They lost their jobs, had their property confiscated, suffered reproach, etc. So Paul challenged the churches in Corinth, Macedonian, Galatia, etc. to come to their aid. Well, the Macedonians came through royally and they were the least likely people that you would expect to respond with such generosity because they had such great need themselves.

Overflowing Joy—Are You Kidding?

I know what you might be thinking about now because I think that too. How is it possible to experience overflowing joy in the middle of trials and what does it mean? Can grace really do that?

Richard Wurmbrand, a Jewish Christian pastor, who later went on to found Voice of the Martyrs shares one of his memories from a time in jail when he and his fellow prisoners underwent great suffering, yet overflowed with joy.

"It was strictly forbidden to preach to other prisoners. It was understood that whoever was caught
doing this received a severe beating. A number
of us decided to pay the price for the privilege of
preaching, so we accepted their terms. It was a
deal; we preached and they beat us. We were happy
preaching. They were happy beating us, so everyone
was happy."[41]

We are to appraise our trials as joy...not because they are joyful
in themselves. Certainly not. Hebrews 12:11 reminds us that all
discipline (literally, "child training") seems painful rather than
pleasant at the moment. When it is coming at you head on and
full-tilt, believe me, it is no fun. But we appraise trials as joy because
of what is coming in the end. Trials yield the peaceful fruit of righteousness. That's God's plan. Moyter cautions us about working up
a fake joy though when he says,

"The meaning of life is not a clue unveiled to James,
but a truth common among Christians—at least as
he sees it—for he says you know (in James 1:3). He
appeals, therefore, not for the adoption of a super-
ficial gaiety in the face of life's adversities, but for a
candid awareness of truth already known."[42]

The Macedonians had learned that this is the only way forward.
Having been given great grace by God for their trials, they could
joyfully and enthusiastically give out of their poverty because they
knew and believed what was yet to come for them. God's plan was
good. They counted on the presence of sufficient grace to get them
through. Paul learned that God's grace was enough:
"My grace is sufficient for you..." (2 Cor. 12:9).

So overflowing joy is possible anywhere, under any experience.

"Count it all joy, my brothers, when you meet trials of various kinds, for you know that the testing of your faith produces steadfastness. And let steadfastness have its full effect, that you may be perfect and complete, lacking in nothing" (James 1:2–4).

This text reminds us that God brings difficulties into our lives for a purpose, and that purpose can be accomplished only if we respond in the right way to our trials. If we believe our trials have as their aim to produce something good, then we can respond with not just joy but overflowing joy.

The joy prescription for trial management is carefully spelled out for us: "Count it all joy when you fall into various trials...." The word *count* refers to the importance which we give to something. It means to have a settled conviction about something.

For instance, in Philippians 3:7–8, Paul counts everything as loss in respect of the glory of knowing Christ. Peter, in 2 Peter 3:15, urges us to count the seeming delay in the return of Christ as a sign of the Lord's patience.

A Change of Thinking

Because we don't naturally think this way, we must allow the Holy Spirit to retrain our thinking about grace in our trials. That's what Peter was after when he told the suffering saints, "Beloved, do not be surprised [don't think it strange] at the fiery trial when it comes upon you to test you, as though something strange were happening to you. But rejoice insofar as you share Christ's sufferings, that you may also rejoice and be glad when his glory is revealed" (1 Pet. 4:12–13).

Peter says glory is coming. And grace will get you there. So change the way you think. Trials are not unexpected, strange things that just pop into the life of the believer. They are "planned excursions" by our life-director- God Himself. Life is not out of control. We are in the company of our Savior in a unique way. We share in His sufferings, and that is part of God's beautiful design. Just knowing this is meant to create joy in us and at the same time bring incredible comfort (2 Cor. 1:5; Phil. 3:10). What a privilege to be in such high company.

We need to have a settled conviction of joy, and then actually engage in rejoicing. But do we ever really do that? This requires a revolution in our thinking and a revision of our spiritual expectations.

The road we are on is both uphill and thorny. The benefits God promises are hard won and the progress painfully made. We must ask the Lord to reform the way we think and the expectations we hold. If our aim is to know and follow Christ and lead others to do that, then we have to know He thought this way too. Hebrews 12:1–2 reminds us of this truth: "Therefore, since we are surrounded by so great a cloud of witnesses, let us also lay aside every weight, and sin which clings so closely, and let us run with endurance the race that is set before us, looking to Jesus, the founder and perfecter of our faith, who for the joy that was set before him endured the cross, despising the shame, and is seated at the right hand of the throne of God."

We have a desperate need for endurance when we suffer.

"The testing of your faith produces steadfastness" (i.e. endurance) (James 1:3). (By the way, this is the same word used in Hebrews 12:2—endured the cross). You see, Jesus thought differently. His expectations were in line with the will of God for His life mission. And that should be true of us also.

The Macedonian folk had their thinking in line with that of Jesus and Paul. The Bible tells us that though Jesus was rich, for our sakes he became poor that we through his poverty might become rich (2 Cor. 8:9). And we know what kind of a stewardship giver Jesus was (and still is). Paul knew what it was like to be poor and to be well-off too. His confession was that he learned contentment in each circumstance (Phil. 4:12). And we know that Paul was a good stewardship manager. (See 2 Cor. 9:12–18 and 2 Cor. 11:7–9.)

There is another mark of God's grace we see on the Macedonian believers.

Mark # 3: God's grace made them just plain generous folk in spite of their poverty.

Let's reset the picture. The reality was that the Macedonians were genuinely poor folk. And on top of that they were greatly afflicted. They were laboring under a double burden. They had very little of the things in this life, and they were going through heavy trial. Yet their extreme poverty was turned into an overflowing wealth of generosity.

Poverty often deepens the trials of a believer. We are not used to thinking of generosity and poverty in the same category, because poverty seems to give a bye in our minds to those thus afflicted. And especially is this true if they are undergoing even more hardship on top of the poverty.

2 Corinthians 8:2 records an amazing paradox for us: "For in a severe test of affliction, their abundance of joy and their extreme poverty have overflowed in a wealth of generosity on their part."

Notice the strangeness of the context here. In light of their generous giving you just don't expect to be told that they are poor. We associate giving with people who can afford to give, especially by our standards of economic ability. But here you have people giving out of their poverty...extreme poverty no less. Notice all the extreme words Paul uses to describe their situation:

- Great testing 2 Corinthians 8:2
- Abundance of their joy 2 Corinthians 8:2
- Extreme poverty 2 Corinthians 8:2

- Wealth of generosity (This word means literally simplicity and singleness of heart, a genuine concern with no hypocrisy attached to it—2 Cor. 8:2).

What do these words tell us?

First, they tell us that these folk knew what it was to suffer, as did their brothers in Christ.

"For you, brothers, became imitators of the churches of God in Christ Jesus that are in Judea. For you suffered the same things from your own countrymen as they did from the Jews..." (1 Thess. 2:14).

Second, these words tell us that these believers practiced an overflowing generosity. Notice Paul does not speak in terms of how much they gave in dollars and cents. He does not do what Judas did when he calculated Mary's gift and how much it could have been sold for. Rather, Paul says from a background of harassment and hard-times these believers were eager to come forward with what they could do. They gave us an incredible legacy of an overflow of generosity.

Andy Stanley speaks of a "legacy of generosity" in his book *How to be Rich* in describing the first century church:

> "Generosity was nothing short of the hallmark of the first-century church. It was all they had. And it proved to be more influential than any amount of money or political sway."[43]

He goes on to tell the story from antiquity about a man named Pachomius.

He was twenty years old when the Romans took over the town of Thebes, where he lived. Pachomius's parents were both pagans, and he considered that to be his lot in life as well. But when the Romans came to town, the course of his life changed forever. When the Roman Empire took over a community, they collected all the young men and drafted them into the Roman army. And because the Roman generals knew these men would escape if possible, they locked them in prison until they could be carted off and trained to serve. While Pachomius was in prison, a famine ravaged the area. Everyone in the prison began to starve. But as Pachomius documents, strangers began to show up at night and slip food between the bars. Night after night, the mysterious people came back. And each time they did, the prisoners inhaled the morsels without asking questions. As a result, Pachomius and his friends survived the horrible famine.

When it was over, Pachomius began to ask questions. Who were those people? Where did they come from, and most of all, why in the world were they feeding us? The answer bewildered him. The strangers were members of the group known as Christians, Galileans, or followers of The Way. When Pachomius completed his obligations to the Roman infantry, he immediately sought out the Christians. From them he learned about Jesus, the resurrection, and the people who now carried out his legacy. Pachomius became a Christian and eventually was a great leader in the early church.[44]

The Macedonians were like those believers.

James M. Boice describes believers as people who think about others even though they themselves are suffering:

> "Unlike other people, when Christians go through
> trials they think about others, who are also suf-
> fering, and they reach out to them."[45]

One of the greatest examples of thinking about others in the throes of great trial is our own Lord Jesus Himself. When he was dying on the cross, He thought of the soldiers. He prayed that the Father would forgive them (Luke 23:34). When he saw his mother in the crowd, he told John, in essence, to take care of her (John 19:26). And remember what he said to the thief dying next to him on the cross? He said "I tell you the truth, today you will be with me in paradise" (Luke 23:43). This selfless, overflowing generosity towards others when we ourselves are suffering is a mark of the life of Christ living through us.

The Macedonian people exercised this overflowing generosity brought on by God's grace as if they were rich people.

Now to be sure it was a generosity that was according to their means. To understand the term *means*, Stanley reminds us that we who live in the US are really rich. It is all a matter of perspective:

> "Our culture's incessant messages about how to get rich (which is off base) because in fact, most of us got rich a long time ago and nobody told us."[46]

You see what the Macedonians did was not so much concern themselves with deciding what to do with their money, but what their money was going to do to them and with them. Their money and resources never owned them nor possessed them. That's why affliction did not derail their sense of stewardship. They could line up with Job who said: "The Lord gave and the Lord took away, blessed be the name of the Lord" (Job 1:21).

Money was not the main focus of their generosity in their trial. Rather it is the activity of God's grace that enabled them to release what they had. They were learning to live in the overflow of grace.

The Bible also makes it clear that theirs was a generosity that was beyond their means too.

Gallup conducted a poll to see how different socioeconomic groups defined *rich*. Not surprisingly, everybody had a different definition—and nobody thought he fit it. Here is what they discovered: For each and every person, "rich" was roughly double the amount possessed by the person defining it. So if a person made $35,000 per year, rich would be someone making at least double that, etc.[47]

Money magazine asked its readers how much money it would take to make them feel rich. Answer? Five million in liquid assets. Based on the trend if you asked people with 5 million to define rich it would be people with ten million.[48]

So it is not in what you have, but in what you do with what you have that makes the difference. Stanley went on to observe:

> "'Rich' is a moving target. No matter how much money we have or make, we will probably never consider ourselves rich. The biggest challenge facing rich people is that they've lost their ability to recognize that they're rich."[49]

There is yet another mark impressed on the Macedonians by God's grace.

Mark # 4: God's grace moved them to give themselves away first. There is even more to their story. 2 Corinthians 8:2–5 says that they gave themselves first. Stewardship is not just about the money you give. It is about a whole life on the line. Stewardship is about giving yourself first.

They were completely willing to participate in this suggestion of Paul to take an offering for their suffering brothers. Why? Because God's grace prompted them to give themselves away first.

Stewardship is not just about the money you give. It is about a whole life on the line. Stewardship is about giving yourself first.

In Jesus' trial on the cross, He gave Himself away. You do not lose when you give yourself away, because that's Christ-like stewardship.

In light of their actions, Paul wanted Titus to urge the

Corinthians, who had a lot more and who were not in such dire straits, to come through in their giving as well. If anyone could be generous it was the Corinthians—yet they were reluctant because they had trouble giving themselves away first. (Sometimes I have learned that the most generous people in our church are those who have the least. Giving is not a problem for them because they have already given themselves away).

As we think about the Macedonians' testimony the question comes to mind about how grace worked to produce this kind of response in them. And will it do the same for us?

Peter teaches us there is a match game going on with our trials. God's grace is equal to all we are facing.

Peter speaks of "various or manifold trials" in I Peter 1:6: "In this you rejoice, though now for a little while, if necessary, you have been grieved by various trials." Then, later in his letter, he speaks in I Peter 4:10 of "God's varied grace...." It is the same word. "As each has received a gift, use it to serve one another, as good stewards of God's varied grace."

These words *various, manifold, varied* (same word) literally mean "multicolored." Some of our trials are dark, heavy trials—and to match those God gives us heavy, corresponding grace. Lighter trials are matched by lighter grace. In other words, for every trial God matches grace, favor, undeserved blessing, strength—whatever we need to get through it and become more like Jesus.

It is not without significance that Peter tells us how we use and handle the grace of God in our lives is a stewardship. It is the management of God's property, which in this case is His grace (1 Pet. 4:10).

Paul reminds us there is a sufficiency about grace when it comes to our trials. God's grace will always be enough and provide enough. Paul's confession of God's sufficient grace toward him in 2

Corinthians 12:7–10 is very comforting and revealing: "My grace is sufficient for you...my strength is made perfect in weakness."

Notice his response to all of this: "Most gladly therefore will I glory in my infirmity [trial] that the power of Christ may rest on me."

There is that rejoicing thing again. What we learn here is this: The grace of God at work in us moves us to joyfully give and serve in spite of whatever affliction may be dogging our steps at the time. The same grace was at work in Corinth.

For you know the grace of our Lord Jesus Christ that though he was rich, yet for your sake he became poor, so that you by his poverty might become rich" (2 Cor. 8:9).

It is unfortunate that we allow ourselves to be blinded to the ongoing expression of God's grace to us. Paul reminded Titus and his people that God's grace is like a training program that molds us into self-controlled, upright and godly people. It equips us to resist ungodly and worldly attitudes and actions (Titus 2:11–12).

The final mark of grace bestowed on the Macedonians is indeed encouraging for all of us to see.

Mark # 5: God's grace provided abundantly for them in spite of their situation.

These Macedonians were provided-for folk.

In spite of their affliction, God's grace abundantly provided for the Macedonian believers so that they lived an overflowing sort of life.

"For in a severe test of affliction, their abundance of joy and their extreme poverty have overflowed in a wealth of generosity on their part. For they gave according to their means, as I can testify, and beyond their means, of their own accord, begging us earnestly for the favor of taking part in the relief of the saints—and this, not as we expected, but they gave themselves first to the Lord and then by the will of God to us" (2 Cor. 8:2–5).

This overflowing of a wealth of generosity points to the gracious provision of God. If you know the Lord, be reminded that God is a provider. He provides for His own. Take the matter of water.

The Shepherd provides water for His sheep in three ways (Ps. 23). First, He gives them dew water. When water is scare, he will take them to some green pasture where there is fresh dew and in that place their needs are met.

Second, he gives them well water. He will take them to a well and draw water out and put it in front of them so they are restored.

Third, he gives them still water. He leads them to a stream of running water, and then dams it up so the water is still, and the sheep are not frightened to drink from it.

In Issac Watts's little known hymn "My Shepherd, You Supply My Need" (based on Psalm 23) he mentions the kind and generous provisions of our Shepherd:

My Shepherd, You supply my need;
most holy is Your name.
In pastures fresh You make me feed,
beside the living stream
You bring my wand'ring spirit back
when I forsake Your ways,
And lead me, for Your mercy's sake,
in paths of truth and grace.

When I walk through the shades of death,
Your presence is my stay;
One word of Your supporting breath
drives all my fears away.
Your hand, in sight of all my foes,
does still my table spread;
My cup with blessings overflows,

Your oil anoints my head.

The sure provisions of my God,
attend me all my days;
Oh, may Your house be my abode
and all my work be praise.
Here would I find a settled rest,
while others go and come.
No more a stranger or a guest
but like a child at home.[50]

That's why believers in the early church were known for their generosity and kindness. They experienced God's provision while their lives were being dismantled by persecution and heartache and yet somehow they managed to be generous (Acts 2:32–37). By the way, this is a far cry from what the "Prosperity Gospel Boys" would have us believe. God did not make these believers materially rich, but rich in grace so they had all they needed to serve their fellow believers and their own needs as well.

Overflowing Generosity Feels No Pressure

It's important to note that the overflowing generosity of the Macedonians was not coerced but freely exercised (2 Cor. 8:3b). This is especially important when we are experiencing great trial. We could feel guilty about not giving of ourselves and means to others.

World War II history relates some very graphic episodes of true voluntary generosity in the midst of great trouble. Most of us have heard of or even seen the film *Bridge over the River Kwai*. The film portrays the brutal treatment of prisoners of war forced by the Japanese to construct a railway line through the Thai jungle. Ernest Gordon's autobiography called *Miracle on the River Kwai* tells an extraordinary tale of survival in those prison camps. In this book he relates the true account of a group of POWs working on the Burma Railway during WW II. Two amazing stories surfaced out of those horrible conditions.

> "At the end of each day the tools were collected from the work part. On one occasion a Japanese guard shouted that a shovel was missing and demanded to know which man had taken it. He began to rant and rave, working himself up into a paranoid fury and ordered whoever was guilty to step forward. No one moved. 'All die. All die,' he shrieked, cocking and aiming his rifle at the prisoners. At that moment one man stepped forward and the guard clubbed him to death with his rifle while he stood silently to attention. When they returned to camp, the tools were counted again and no shovel was missing."[51]

No one forced that man to make the sacrifice. Some would have called him foolish. Yet it was a voluntary sacrifice, a freely offered generosity on the behalf of another. In the midst of his own struggle, he served another.

Another story that came to light concerned a man named Angus. It was the custom among the Argyll's for every man to have a "mucker," that is, a pal or friend with whom he shared or "mucked in" everything he had. An Argyll called Angus had a mucker who became very ill. It seemed pretty certain to everyone that he was going to die. Certain, that is, to everyone but Angus. When someone stole his mucker's blanket Angus gave him his own. Every mealtime Angus would draw his ration only to give it to his friend. Perhaps you can guess the end of the story. The mucker got better.

But Angus collapsed, and died caused by starvation and exhaustion. He did it all for his friend. "Greater love hath no man than this, that a man lay down his life for his friends" (John 15:13). The story of Angus's sacrifice spread through the camp affecting everyone.[52]

Yet what these men did illustrates what the Macedonian's did in the middle of their trial. They gave themselves first to the Lord and then gave other things. They did so freely with no emotional or mental pressure applied to them.

This was a generosity that flowed out of the way they managed all of their lives (2 Cor. 8:4–5). It seems that people who get rich suddenly, struggle to manage everything in their lives well. I read recently that according to Sports Illustrated an amazing 78 percent of NFL players find themselves bankrupt or financially stressed within two years of retirement. And 60 percent of NBA players are broke within five years of walking off the court. It is no better with lottery winners. Nearly half of them had spent their entire winnings within five years and some even had to declare bankruptcy.[53]

Trials Are No Excuse for Not Giving

There are three flaws that can enter our thinking when we connect giving with our trials.

1: I must not think that giving is a means of making my trial go away. It is not a bargaining chip I use with God. We cannot solve the issue of our suffering by giving. I must not think if I give of myself or my means that God will say, "Hey, that's good. Poof. Your trial is gone." The Macedonians were not bargaining with God for release from their prison of suffering by giving. Even the amount we give must not be viewed as some kind of

> *Remember, giving is never an end in itself. It is the expression of other things at work in my life.*

payment that will remove the suffering I am experiencing. Remember, giving is never an end in itself. It is the expression of other things at work in my life.

2: I must not think that my trial is an excuse for me to cease giving of myself and my means to God. It is true in a trial you may not have a lot of resources or even the mental and emotional health to give like you wish you could. But we must guard against excusing ourselves from giving because we have a trial going on. Certainly the Macedonians refused to walk down that path.

> "We must believe generosity is a spiritual experience well before it is a financial decision....Generosity is not something God wants from us. It's something God wants for us."[54]

Think about this: if God has you, then your offerings, your time, your resources and your energy are not an issue. If God truly has you, then He already has those things. Giving becomes joyful and desirable when you have given yourself. It seems then, the measure of our devotion to Christ can be found in how easy or difficult, or how joyful or painful the giving portion of our lives seems to be. And the test of the reality of our Christianity often shows up when it is the hardest to give.

3: I must not think that giving in the midst of my trial is optional. I am cut from a bolt of cloth marked by giving no matter what is transpiring in my life. Christ's giving flowed out of who He knew He was. Paul makes an interesting statement about Jesus in relation to this:

"He never grasped after being God with all its privileges" (Phil. 2:6).

Why was He not grasping after this position? He already had that. So the acts of giving, humbling, and even dying flowed out of who He was without any effort or grasping. The greatest giving of our Savior was in the midst of his greatest trial—dying on the cross for our sins. That's what it should be for us who know and follow Christ. Giving flows out of who we are even if we are experiencing trials. Trials cannot change who we are.

Understanding God's Generosity

If we are to be generous in trial then we must understand how God displays His generosity to us in those moments.

Now the word *generosity* has a strange literal meaning. It is the word for "a single or sound eye." How did it come to mean generosity? There are two ideas in this word:

[1] There is the idea of selflessness. This speaks of single-minded concern for the other person.
[2] There is also the idea of exclusive pre-occupation. This speaks of a mind set upon just one task as if there were nothing else to do.

This is how the giving God gives...with a selfless, total concern for us and with an exclusive preoccupation as if He had nothing else to do but to give to us and give again (James 1:5). What a comfort in difficulty. And what an incentive for prayer and for asking wisdom from such a God.

When you are in the midst of some trial, giving is never easy. But grace is present and wisdom is available.

Asking for wisdom from God is to see and understand the possibilities of prayer. We will either come to God with faith or with doubt (James 1:6–7). Are we wholeheartedly committed to His way of seeing things and His ambitions for our future?

Do we believe He is outrageously generous? Or are we trying to have our foot in each camp? This divided heart (two-souled) way of thinking brings instability to us in the middle of our trials (James 1:8) unless we believe that God will do as He promised.

When you are in the midst of some trial, giving is never easy. But grace is present and wisdom is available. Managing your trials as a good steward requires us to be generous in a time when generosity is probably the last thing on our minds.

Can Trials Produce Generosity in Us?

Managed trials can only produce life generosity if certain conditions are met.

1: Trials can produce generosity only if our hope is in eternal life not temporary life.

James 1:9–11 presents contrasting circumstances of life to us. There is the lowly brother. This is one who is economically poor but who is a committed believer.

And then there is the rich brother. This is one who is economically comfortable, but perhaps just as committed as the poor brother.

The wisdom of God penetrates below what you see on the surface to the reality of what really exists.

All of us have trials no matter what our economic status in life may be. The poor man should rejoice even if he has little. The rich man should be sobered and humbled even if he has a lot. Both should live and think in light of eternity. All of us must learn to see ourselves in the light of God's reality for us. That's why James 1:11 is so important for us to understand.

"For the sun rises with its scorching heat and withers the grass; its flower falls, and its beauty perishes. So also will the rich man fade away in the midst of his pursuits."

The wisdom of God penetrates below what you see on the surface to the reality of what really exists. He gives us a comparison when he says that riches and those who hold them are like flowers. They don't last. They will instead wilt, fade, and ultimately die.

"And the rich in his humiliation, because like a flower of the grass he will pass away" (James 1:10b).

One can have too much dependence upon favorable circumstances and too much helplessness in the face of adverse conditions.

> *The person whose whole way of life is in what he can own, possess, and earn has no security.*

The person whose whole way of life is in what he can own, possess, and earn has no security. He will fade, fall, wither, and perish. Ominous words, are they not? Why? Because all that he has is at the mercy of circumstance.

Is wealth wrong? *No.* But the Bible tells us it is all in how it has been acquired, how it is used, and what place it holds in the heart of the one who possesses it.

2: Trials can produce generosity only if we remain faithful under trial.

We must commit to be faithful no matter what our economic condition because we know that tomorrow will be better than today. In James 1:12 we read:

"Blessed is the man who remains steadfast under trial, for when he has stood the test he will receive the crown of life, which God has promised to those who love him."

If we endure trial then the promise stands that we will ultimately receive blessing. Enduring trials brings not blight, but blessing. Maybe not all in this life, but it will come.

This paradox of being tried and yet experiencing blessing in the trial is a strange one. We are told that the man who endures and remains faithful when he is tried is blessed. The word "blessed" has two basic meanings. It means "happy" in a general sense (Acts 26:2; Rom. 14:22). In a specific sense it means "fulfilled" (Luke 12:37; see Matt. 5:3ff in the beatitudes). This "better-tomorrow-blessing" has to do with something called "the crown of life" that comes to the suffering believer.

In the Bible, the wearing of a crown for the believer speaks of several things:

#1—It speaks of the honor of position (Esther 8:15; Ps. 21:3).
#2—It speaks of a joyful outcome and a glorious conclusion (1 Thess. 2:19; Song of Sol. 3:11).
#3—It speaks of a sure victory (1 Cor. 9:25).
#4—It speaks of the reward when the race ends (2 Tim. 4:8).
#5—It speaks of the chief shepherd's reward to his under shepherds (1 Pet. 5:4).
#6—It speaks specifically of the reward for faithfulness (Rev. 2:10).

The crown James speaks of goes to those who were faithful because they loved the Lord.

Endurance brings blessing. And God's blessing releases us to be generous with others. This principle is critical to managing our trials as good stewards of God for it brings us hope in the face of the inevitability of trials. If trials are woven by God into our lives for His good purposes, then we must receive them and manage them with His strength knowing a blessing is waiting for us in the future. I can give generously when I know what I know.

I remember a funny little story about a woman who dearly loved her cat. Her husband did not share her love for this creature. It became necessary for the wife to take a trip out of town for a few days, so while she was gone, the husband took the cat, put it in a bag and threw it in the river (apologies to cat lovers). When his wife returned, of course she could not find her cat. Her husband played dumb about its whereabouts. She was depressed and her husband told her because he loved her he would take out a full page ad in the city newspaper with the cat's picture and description and a reward of five thousand dollars for its return. She was thrilled with his generous act on behalf of her cat. When the man went to work, some of his coworkers questioned him about offering such a generous reward for the cat. This was his response: "When you know what I know, you can afford to be generous." That's how we can be generous. We know things.

This is what Peter meant when he said in I Peter 1:7:

"So that the tested genuineness of your faith—more precious than gold that perishes though it is tested by fire—may be found to result in praise and glory and honor at the revelation of Jesus Christ." That is what we know. Our generosity flows out of the promise God makes regarding how our trials end up!

Warnings and Blessings

Warning:

When we have days without difficulties, we can easily allow our love for the Lord to diminish (Proverbs 30:8, 9). So to keep that love alive, God intersperses trials into our path. These trials have a way of keeping us close to Him and in love with Him. The Macedonians seemed to have that love for the Lord. In their trials, there was joy, trouble, generosity, poverty all mixed together to produce people who received grace and reward from the Lord as they remained faithful.

Blessing:

Our experience of God's grace comes alive when we come to know Jesus Christ as our Savior. Because sin has brought nothing but death and heartache to us, we desperately need a Savior. The grace of God brings Jesus to us. (Eph. 2:8–9). And the coming of Jesus into the life results in the greatest blessing of all.

> "The choice is this: live or die, know him or else. Be forgiven by the wonder of what Christ did for you, or receive what you've done fair and square on your own head.... Outside of Christ, life takes place in the black hole of sin and misery. It's dangerous—damnable—to live outside the grace of God. If you are in your sins, not in Christ, you are dead (Eph. 2:1). Though the devil doesn't make you do it, he's got you dancing to his tune (2:2)."[55]

Yet we are not done with grace after our salvation. Our trials serve to convince us that God's grace is sufficient for us just as it was for Paul and for all of the believers who have gone before us.

Acquiring Stewardship Strategies in Our Trials

If grace is to help us live as did our Macedonian friends in the midst of their afflictions, then we must develop three basic stewardship strategies during our own trials.

First, let the Spirit of God change the way you think. Proverbs 23:7 reminds us that the way we think is really the way we are. I must embrace in my thinking the fact that trials are planned events. I must not think of them as some strange or out- of-control experiences that come charging in on me unchecked. Relax. God knows. God will give grace to me during these very moments. His plans for us are always accompanied by grace (Acts 9:16; 2 Cor. 12:7–9).

Second, remember that generosity will never be convenient and comfortable. If we are to be generous stewards over all that God has given us, then we must not let our trials short-circuit our giving. Sometimes God uses our generosity in suffering to float an unexpected blessing our way. God never promises riches or comfort will be ours, but God does promise that His faithfulness and grace will sustain us and encourage us when we need it most. The Macedonians flourished by grace in the midst of their poverty and suffering as they gave of themselves and their resources to others. Joy was their blessing.

> *Taking the quick fix often compounds and complicates our trials and puts us in the driver's seat of our own journey. We are not wise enough to navigate the path of a quick fix.*

"Grace not only frees us from our sins, it also frees us from ourselves. The grace of God will open our heart and our hand. Our giving will not be the result of cold calculation, but of warm-hearted jubilation."[56]

Third, do not be pressured (by your own heart or by others' advice) into easy solutions. Some trials are designed by God to go the distance in order to make us more like Jesus and develop in us a Christ-like character that brings rich fruit and ultimate reward. Remember, God *will* fix it ultimately in His time and in His way. Taking the quick fix often compounds and complicates our trials and puts us in the driver's seat of our own journey. We are not wise enough to navigate the path of a quick fix. Now God can and sometimes does bring about an immediate solution. But let it be His solution, not your own forced fix.

Study Guide Questions

1. It seems that trials are not subject to easy fixes. What are some "easy fixes" that many seek when suffering a trial? Why are those fixes ineffective? Do this fixes mitigate against our stewardship or enhance it?

2. What are some excuses we use for not being generous when we are experiencing some life difficulty? What does this tell us about our understanding of the grace of God and our own exercise of faith?

3. Would you consider yourself rich? What factors do you use to evaluate whether you are rich or poor? Should your economic status affect your management of your trials, and if so in what way?

4. Name some joy killers that come to the surface when you are suffering a hard patch of life? Why is it that we are sometimes reluctant to try God's solutions for restoring our joy in our trials?

5. Why do we give so little time thinking about the rewards God has promised us for faithful stewardship? Which world reality most dominates our thinking and actions and how do we retrain our thinking toward heavenly rewards vs. earthly troubles?

Chapter Four

Focused:
Text: 1 Peter 1:6–8

I read somewhere recently an article[57] that speaks about how a pastor knows a trial is about to happen:

- You go into the pulpit, look down and notice that you have last week's sermon notes
- Your youth pastor urgently asks you about the church's liability insurance
- Your church treasurer asks you just before the annual meeting if the copier will copy in red
- You are informed that the youth group accidently used steel wool sponges for their free neighborhood car wash.
- You and your wife are the only ones at the pot-luck dinner
- You get a letter from the city that they have designated the lot across the street from your church as a landfill site.
- You are assigned to nursery duty during the morning service.

We chuckle at these funny scenarios but in reality, trials are no laughing matter for a pastor or anyone else in the congregation.

In this chapter we want to bring together and reflect on what we have learned about trials and stewardship on our journey together thus far. It is just here that we need to acquire a determined focus in our trials that will yield good stewardship for God's glory.

I love the response of a soldier who was recounting a tough battle experience in which he and his buddies were outnumbered and hard pressed. Someone asked him this question: "What did you do?" This was his answer: "We were so outnumbered there was only one thing to do. We attacked."

Talk about focus. We are just going to fight. Period.

The Next Play

I believe that one of the biggest hurdles in all of our trials and struggles is to respond in the way God tells us we should. But it is not easy to get back up and refocus when you have been laid low by a trial. It is not easy to embrace God's take on our trials and joyfully muddle on with a clear focus.

Joe Namath, the famous former quarterback for the New York Jets used to say, after being tackled, "By the time I'm climbing back up from going down, I'm already thinking about the next play."

Let's go back to 1 Peter chapter 1 and think about the next play. In this epistle, Peter is writing to Christians that were spread throughout Asia Minor, which is modern-day Turkey. They had been scattered because of the persecution coming from Rome. These believers were being persecuted for following Christ and they were being persecuted because following Christ made them different. He writes to encourage them:

"In this you greatly rejoice, though now for a little while you may have had to suffer grief in all kinds of trials" (1 Pet. 1:6).

Peter says it is possible for believers to have both great joy and real grief in the midst of their trials. The words of this verse can also be translated as a command: "Rejoice in this." These believers were suffering through all kinds of trials, yet they had joy.

As we look at Scripture, we see that Peter is not the only writer who teaches this apparent paradox. Paul, in fact, lived it.

"Sorrowful, yet always rejoicing; poor, yet making many rich; having nothing, and yet possessing everything" (2 Cor. 6:10).

These texts lead us to ask a very searching question: Can joy and pain realistically coexist in the life of a believer?

Can Joy and Pain Coexist?

Paul said he was at the same time sorrowful and still rejoicing. To have joy in trials is not to deny pain. It is to recognize the fact that they can exist together. They can coexist in the same way an expectant mother can go through the agony of giving birth and still have joy in thinking about what is to come. She has joy because she has the right focus as she considers this new baby that will be birthed into the world (John 16:21-22).

> *We have to learn to focus outside of the trial itself and even to focus beyond the trial. That is the key. If the trial itself consumes our focus, joy will never come to us, and we will fail in the stewardship of our trials.*

How can we live this type of joy/pain kind of experience as believers who want to steward well God's property? Trials will be our lot. That's where we will live off and on all our lives. May I suggest that it is a matter of a learned focus. We have to learn to focus outside of the trial itself and even to focus beyond the trial. That is the key. If the trial itself consumes our focus, joy will never come to us, and we will fail in the stewardship of our trials.

George Muller, of Bristol, who was mightily used of God to establish orphanages that were run purely by faith, was on a ship headed to Quebec. They ran into heavy fog that was delaying the arrival time to their destination. Mr. Muller always honored his speaking engagements by being on time, so he told the captain of the ship that he wanted to pray about the problem, so he could still make it to his destination to honor his commitment. The captain said to him, "Mr. Muller, do you know how dense this fog is?"

Mr. Muller replied, "No, my eye is not on the density of the fog, but on the living God who controls every circumstance of my life."[58] He refused to focus on the trial itself but instead chose to look outside of it to the God who controls all things, even fog.

Peter gets us outside of our trials. He tells us where to put our focus and when we learn to do that, we become good stewards of our trials, and joy becomes a real response.

Where should we start? This might be painful to hear, but we have to learn some focus lessons.

Focus on the Past—Our Salvation

We must focus on the benefits of our salvation in Christ. This is our first lesson.

This is where Peter takes us when he says:

"In this you greatly rejoice, though now for a little while you may have had to suffer grief in all kinds of trials" (1 Pet. 1:6).

What is Peter referring to when he says "in this" you greatly rejoice? In the flow of thought, "this" points back to our new birth (1 Pet. 1:3–5). Listen to what he says in the previous verses: "Praise be to the God and Father of our Lord Jesus Christ. In his great mercy he has given us new birth into a living hope through the resurrection of Jesus Christ from the dead, and into an inheritance that can never perish, spoil or fade—kept in heaven for you, who through faith are shielded by God's power until the coming of the salvation that is ready to be revealed in the last time" (1 Pet. 1:3–5).

Peter says we have been given a new birth into a living hope through the living Christ. Did you pick up on those words in verse 3?

"Blessed be the God and Father of our Lord Jesus Christ. According to his great mercy, he has caused us to be born again to a living hope through the resurrection of Jesus Christ from the dead" (1 Pet. 1:3).

We focus on the fact that we are new people in Christ and we are not the same anymore. There was a time when we were dead to God, but now we are alive to him. We are alive to his Word and alive to one another, where before we were dead in trespasses and sins (Eph. 2:1–5). This is something we can rejoice in even in the midst of trials.

Only those who understand the truth that God keeps the salvation of every believer can truly rejoice and maintain the right focus. Some believers have lost their focus or even fallen into spiritual depression thinking they have sinned in such a way that they have forfeited their salvation. The Bible clearly teaches that if you are truly born again, you are kept by God's power until the coming of Christ.

"Who by God's power are being guarded through faith for a salvation ready to be revealed in the last time" (1 Pet. 1:5).

You are not now, nor ever were, nor ever will be kept by the power of your faith or the diligence of your effort.

God is the one who gives you faith (Ephesians 2:8, 9), and He is the one who does the work of keeping it.

Take the promise of Romans 8:28: "And we know that for those who love God all things work together for good for those who are called according to his purpose."

This is only true if our salvation is secure. Only then can all things work together for the good of those who love the Lord. And you will want to notice the word *together*. It does not mean that God's keeping power will spare you from trouble here. It simply says all the good and all the bad that happens to you works "together" for good.

One of the things we should love about Peter is his focus on the gospel. He brings us back to the basics. He brings us back to our salvation. It's extremely important because it so easy to lose the focus that should be ours. It is the salvation gospel that brings us joy and keeps our focus steady.

Focus on the Future—Our Inheritance

We manage our trials with joy when we learn to focus on our future, indestructible inheritance.

"To an inheritance that is imperishable, undefiled, and unfading kept in heaven for you" (1 Pet. 1:4).

C. S. Lewis felt this longing for our future when he wrote the following:

> "If I find in myself a desire which no experience in
> this world can satisfy, the most probable explana-
> tion is that I was made for another world."[59]

Indeed, we are made for another world with a whole new life made possible by our inheritance.

With this new birth, we receive an inheritance in heaven. Jesus said in his high priestly prayer in John 17:22 that the glory He had in heaven has been shared with us. Romans 8:17 declares that we are coheirs with Christ, and therefore, what is the Son's is ours. In fact, in some way it seems that we benefit from this inheritance now. Ephesians 1:3 says we have every spiritual blessing in heavenly places. Ephesians 2:6 says we are seated in heavenly places with Christ. This means Christ is ruling in heaven but we are there in spirit with him. Everything that's His, is ours. We are coheirs. This is a phenomenal concept.

What this means is that God is preserving this inheritance, keeping it from decay or being stolen, even right now. There are a lot of people in this life who never receive their natural inheritance. Maybe they don't receive it because the inheritance is lost or its value changes. Maybe they did not even get one at all. Or maybe that inheritance was contested by the state, by other relatives or any number of reasons. But the inheritance to which Peter refers can never perish, spoil, fade or be stolen away. God is protecting it for us. That's something we can focus on, even when our natural inheritance is taken away or never realized. So what have we learned? The answer to that very practical question we raised earlier, "How can we manage our trials with joy and a clear focus?" is found right here in the text.

The answer is not complicated according to Peter. He teaches us that we manage our trials by focusing on the benefits of our salvation and the prospect of our inheritance. When we have experienced the new birth, we have an inheritance waiting for us in heaven, and our salvation is eternal because God is preserving it for us. Now managing trials with a determined focus includes another lesson we must learn.

Purpose and Sovereignty in Trial

We must focus on God's sovereignty and purpose in the trial. God affirms his work of sovereignty in the midst of trouble.

"I form light and create darkness; I make well-being and create calamity; I am the LORD, who does all these things" (Isa. 45:7).

God does not ask us to like what He does. But He does require us to acknowledge and trust what He is doing and what He will yet do. God does nothing that is not necessary for us.

"Things happen and events occur because they are the fulfillment of God's plan and purpose.... If God has plans for the future, we shouldn't complain about the present. If we don't like what He is doing in the present, it's because He hasn't yet finished. The present is on its way to the future, and every part of it is under His control."[60]

Peter goes a little further in his teaching on trials in 1 Peter 1:6 when he says God's purposes in trial are necessary for us: "In this you rejoice, though now for a little while, if necessary, you have been grieved by various trials."

We can manage our trials with joy and a clear focus because they have purpose. They are not haphazard, they are not by accident, they are necessary—and God has not forgotten about us. Martyn Lloyd-Jones in one of his writings put it this way:

"It is a fundamental principle in the life and walk of faith that we must always be prepared for the unexpected when we are dealing with God...because God is sovereign, there are no formulas which will ensure that He will work in a particular way."[61]

When Lloyd-Jones himself was experiencing a tough time in ministry his friend Dr. John MacLead wrote these powerful words to him (Lloyd-Jones said that Dr. MacLead was one of the godliest men he had ever met):

"God is mightier than the floods whose tumbling and confused noise may at times test the faith and confidence of God's own people."[62]

Trials Are Necessary Sometimes

"In this you greatly rejoice, though now for a little while if necessary...." (1 Pet. 1:6). Let's think a little more about that necessary thing.

As a father, He only allows us to go through things that are necessary for us. He doesn't waste anything. This is one of the major reasons we must not lose our focus in the midst of trials. It is this way with any good father. A good father only allows his child to go through trials if they are necessary for him.

> *We can manage our trials with joy and a clear focus because they have purpose. They are not haphazard, they are not by accident, they are necessary—and God has not forgotten about us.*

The son wants to quit baseball because he's not very good, but the father knows that the discipline and perseverance he is developing is needed for whatever career God leads him into. So the father makes the child finish the season only because it's necessary for his growth. The child may cry and complain, and it is not that the father is immune to the child's tears, but it is because he knows what's best.

Our Heavenly Father also knows what's best. Listen to what the writer of Hebrews says about trials: "It is for discipline that you have to endure. God is treating you as sons. For what son is there whom his father does not discipline?" (Heb. 12:7).

It may seem strange then to hear God tell us to rejoice in our trials because the trial does not feel like I am loved by my Heavenly Father. I think it is important here to pause and separate the word *rejoice* from the idea of feeling only positive emotions. To rejoice, in this sense, does not necessarily mean to "be happy," as we understand the terms today. While rejoicing may include positive feelings, the New Testament often communicates that rejoicing is a choice about how we think about our lives (James 1:2; Phil. 4:4). It is not rejoicing but necessity that's the object of focus in our trials.

If we buy into the truth that our kind, all-wise Heavenly Father deems that our trial is necessary, and He is treating us as beloved sons, then our focus takes on an entirely different face. There is a relationship involved here…a father and son relationship in which trust and joy can intermingle.

We must conclude then, that this rejoicing is less about feelings and more about a faith focus. It is less about maintaining some perfect emotional state and more about a declaration: "My life is worth rejoicing over because of what God is doing for me right now. He deems this path necessary. I am provided for. My future is secure. Nothing can change that. I am rejoicing because my focus is fixed on God's goodness to me as my Father."

> *God is in control of every hardship a believer goes through and he brings them to us as a loving father to his son.*

That's why the writer of Hebrews says that when you endure hardship as discipline you are assured that God is treating you as sons. The point the author is trying to make is this: God is in control of every hardship a believer goes through and he brings them to us as a loving father to his son. (cf. Eph. 1:11; Rom. 8:28).

Now there are those who struggle with this reality and say, "What about trials that come from Satan or from my own failures?" Yes, God is in control of those trials as well. Paul says the same thing in other texts.

"No temptation has overtaken you that is not common to man. God is faithful, and he will not let you be tempted beyond your ability, but with the temptation he will also provide the way of escape, that you may be able to endure it" (1 Cor. 10:13).

God knows exactly what you need and how much you can handle. Believers can rejoice in trials because of this: they have purpose. That's where we must put our focus.

Focus on this great truth: These trials are necessary for us. The fact that they are necessary means there is "intention" behind them. Reading an article some time ago, I was reminded of some very practical reasons trials are necessary for us as believers[63]

1: Some trials are necessary to turn us away from sin. This is what we see happening to the Corinthians in 1 Corinthians 11. They were abusing the Lord's Supper, and God brought weakness, sickness, and even death on them.

"That is why many of you are weak and ill, and some have died. But if we judged ourselves truly, we would not be judged. But when we are judged by the Lord, we are disciplined so that we may not be condemned along with the world." (1 Cor. 11:30–32).

Sometimes God brings trials to discipline us and to turn us away from sin. Listen to what David said in Psalm 119:67 about his experience with discipline: "Before I was afflicted I went astray, but now I obey your word."

Before discipline came, David was living in sin, but after the affliction, he obeyed God's words.

Death is the ultimate way to turn someone from sin. He did this with Ananias and Sapphira in Acts 5. They were lying to God and before the church about their giving and because of this God took them home.

2: Some trials are necessary to protect us from sin.

Think about Paul and his thorn in the flesh. "So to keep me from becoming conceited because of the surpassing greatness of the revelations, a thorn was given me in the flesh, a messenger of Satan to harass me, to keep me from becoming conceited" (2 Cor. 12:7).

We are not sure what this thorn in the flesh was. God has chosen not to reveal it. Sometimes God is deliberately ambiguous. Perhaps

God did this so that we could apply it to any trial we experience, whether that trial includes sickness, depression, or any number of difficult circumstances. Whatever Paul's trial, it was given to him because of the "surpassing great revelations" he had received from God. In the previous verses (1–6), Paul spoke about how he was taken to heaven and saw visions of things he could not put into words. These heady experiences could make any person proud.

In order to keep him from pride, God humbled Paul through an affliction He allowed Satan to bring. The text does not say that Paul was prideful, but that God was saving him from the sin of pride through this humbling experience.

Many trials we go through could possibly be a form of God's grace to keep us from sin and pride. Charles Spurgeon, who was called the Prince of Preachers, used to struggle with depression that was so bad at times he couldn't leave his bed for weeks. He was a great and successful preacher who addressed crowds of thousands each week, yet this very struggle with depression that Spurgeon endured may have kept him from the Achilles heel of pride.

The trial given to Paul was a work of grace to keep him from the sin of pride.

3: Some trials are needed in order for us to grow in Christ-like character.

"No discipline seems pleasant at the time, but painful. Later on, however, it produces a harvest of righteousness and peace for those who have been trained by it" (Heb. 12:11).

For those who are trained by going through hardship, a harvest of righteousness is produced in their character. Peace, patience, endurance, love, and joy are some of the fruits of trial. There is a harvest for those who have been trained by pain. Look at the life of any truly godly man or woman, and you will see that godliness has always been marked by trials. So we are trained by persevering through the trial and seeking the Lord and his Word in the midst of it.

However, those who are not trained by it often develop strongholds.

"Therefore, strengthen your feeble arms and weak knees. Make level paths for your feet so that the lame may not be disabled, but rather healed" (Heb. 12:12–13).

These strongholds and addictions prevent growth. It is harder for them to love, harder for them to forgive, or harder for them to have peace. They become lame and disabled. Only those who are trained by the trial, develop the character God wants. Here is how one person put it:

"I am progressing along the path of life in my ordinary contented condition, when suddenly a stab of pain threatens serious disease, or a newspaper headline threatens us all with destruction."

"At first I am overwhelmed, and all my little 'happinesses' look like broken toys. And perhaps, by God's grace, I succeed, and for a day or two become a creature consciously dependent on God and drawing its strength from the right sources. But the moment the threat is withdrawn, my whole nature leaps back to the toys."

"Thus the terrible necessity of trials is only too clear. God has had me for but 48 hours and then only by dint of taking everything else away from me. Let Him but sheathe the sword for a minute, and I behave like a puppy when the hated bath is over — I shake myself as dry as I can and race off to reacquire my comfortable dirtiness in the nearest flower bed."

"And that is why trials cannot cease until God sees us remade."

4: Some trials may be necessary in order to further equip us for ministry.

"Who comforts us in all our affliction, so that we may be able to comfort those who are in any affliction, with the comfort with which we ourselves are comforted by God. For as we share abundantly in Christ's sufferings, so through Christ we share abundantly in comfort too. If we are afflicted, it is for your comfort and salvation; and if we are comforted, it is for your comfort, which you experience when you patiently endure the same sufferings that we suffer" (2 Cor. 1:4–6).

Paul learned that God comforted him in the midst of his own trouble so he could comfort those in any trouble. What an outward focus he maintained during his trials. Oswald Chambers observed:

> "If you are going to be used by God, He will take you through a multitude of experiences that are not meant for you at all; they are meant to make you useful in his hands....We are not sanctified for ourselves, we are called into the fellowship of the Gospel, and things happen which have nothing to do with us.... If through a broken heart God can bring His purposes to pass in the world, then thank Him for breaking your heart."[64]

But there are some Christians, especially young Christians, who struggle with how to comfort somebody in the midst of a failure, a loss, or some depression. This is not their fault, and it is not necessarily a lack of spirituality. Many of them just don't have the experience of going through trials with God yet. This is where God prepares His counselors.

Trials Are Not Just about You

One of the wonderful promises about this text is that God uses trouble in order to comfort us so we can comfort those who go through "any trouble" (2 Cor. 1:4). It is not just about me. God has given me gifts to use for the benefit of others, even when I am in the midst of a trial.

"As each has received a gift, use it to serve one another as good stewards of God's varied grace: whoever speaks, as one who speaks oracles of God; whoever serves, as one who serves by the strength that God supplies—in order that in everything God may be glorified through Jesus Christ. To him belong glory and dominion forever and ever. Amen" (I Pet. 5:10–11).

I am to continue serving God and others. I don't get a day off. This means that whatever my trial might be, it can be used to help believers who have experienced trials that are different from mine. I don't necessarily have to experience exactly what they have gone through to comfort them.

> "We do not need to experience exactly the same trials as others in order to be able to share God's encouragement. If we have experienced God's comfort, then 'we can comfort those in any trouble'... Our experiences cannot alter the comfort of God. That remains sufficient and efficient no matter what our own experiences may have been."[65]

Here is how this works. In the midst of pain, God creates a reservoir in you. This reservoir allows you to go deeper than you have before. Psalm 84:6 talks about those who go through the valley of Baca (weeping) and leave a well behind. Those of you who are hard-hearted and never cry, God teaches you to cry through pain. He teaches you to feel the heartaches of others. He teaches you how to better hear God's voice in times of suffering. All of this will enable you, in a special way, to minister to others. David Powlison reminds us of this:

In the midst of pain, God creates a reservoir in you. This reservoir allows you to go deeper than you have before.

"In suffering I learned to need mercy. From suffering, I learned to give mercy."[66]

It is a mystery, but God brings comfort through the broken. It is often through the broken that God pours out His precious grace and mercy into others who hurt.

"God puts you in hard moments when you cry out for his comfort so that your heart becomes tender to those near you who need the same comfort."[67]

Your trial is a "ministry place" from which God displays his grace and power to others who need it too. That's why it is vital to keep your focus in your trials.

Future Reward

A right focus in trials must also include the matter of future glory. Let's go back and think about this future glory thing.

Peter's view of tomorrow is incredible.

"So that the tested genuineness of your faith—more precious than gold that perishes though it is tested by fire—may be found to result in praise and glory and honor at the revelation of Jesus Christ" (1 Pet. 1:7).

The text says that the trials have come so that our faith "may result in praise, glory and honor when Jesus Christ is revealed." This seems to be referring to the reality that God honors you for your faithfulness in going through trials and in some marvelous way, He receives glory in all of this!

Christ taught the same thing.

"Blessed are you when others revile you and persecute you and utter all kinds of evil against you falsely on my account. Rejoice and be glad, for your reward is great in heaven, for so they persecuted the prophets who were before you" (Matt. 5:1–12).

There is a reward given for suffering.

James says the same thing:

"Blessed is the man who perseveres under trial, because when he has stood the test, he will receive the crown of life) that God has promised to those who love him" (James 1:12).

Thinking about the future that God has promised is a lot like when it comes to making out your income taxes. You rejoice at the regular income and the extra income God provides, but have you ever reluctantly given your offering, especially when you have other needs or things you want? Then comes tax time and everything changes. As you figure out your taxes, you flinch at every source of income and rejoice with every tithe and offering you gave. More income, more tax. More offerings, less tax.

Here is a question to ponder: Does simply going through a trial warrant reward in heaven? No, it's *how* we go through the trial that brings the reward. James says blessed, or happy, is the man who perseveres under trial.

Take Israel for example. We see Israel going through trials in the wilderness, and God disciplining them. They fell away from God, they complained about God, and they were divided. There was certainly no reward there. No faith, No reward.

Two Friends: Faith and Trials

Trials and faith are good friends and travel companions. They work well together. The Bible tells us that God rewards those who faithfully persevere.

"Do not be afraid of what you are about to suffer. I tell you, the devil will put some of you in prison to test you, and you will suffer persecution for ten days. Be faithful, even to the point of death, and I will give you the crown of life" (Rev. 2:10).

Did you catch those words of Christ in Revelation 2:10? "Be faithful, even to the point of death, and I will give you the crown of life."

God will honor those who have been faithful in the way they have persevered through trials. They did not become like the Israelites who murmured, gossiped, became divisive, and ultimately turned away from God. Those who are faithful—meaning that they didn't quit, but continued to trust in God and honor him in the midst of trials—will be richly rewarded.

Hebrews 11:6 speaks of these rewards: "And without faith it is impossible to please God, because anyone who comes to him must believe that he exists and that he rewards those who earnestly seek him."

So the question comes to us: Are you faithfully seeking Him in the midst of your trial? God says, "That's what I'm looking for. I will reward those who have faith in the midst of their trials. I will rejoice over them and honor them. I will give them a crown."

Peter saw this and focused on this in the midst of his trials. He also called these suffering saints to focus on it as well.

There is an old spiritual that goes something like this:

One of these days I'm going home where no sorrows ever come
We'll soon be done with troubles and trials
Safe from heartache pain and care we shall all that glory share
Then I'm gonna sit down beside my Jesus, sit down and rest a little while
We'll soon be done with troubles and trials
Yes in that home on the other side. Shake glad hands with the elders, tell my kindred good morning. Sit down beside my Jesus, sit down and rest a little while.

Looking Through the Democrats and Republicans to See Christ

There is one other focus that's crucial to trial management. It involves seeing and knowing Christ better. Peter challenges us to look at our tough circumstances from an entirely different perspective.

"Though you have not seen him, you love him. Though you do not now see him, you believe in him and rejoice with joy that is inexpressible and filled with glory...." (1 Pet. 1:8).

Notice that Peter, in speaking to these Christians, says they are filled with an inexpressible and glorious joy because of their love and belief in Christ. How can this bring joy? It brings joy because it is in the midst of the trial that we see Christ and know Him better. It is this loving and joyful relationship with Christ that allows us to endure and manage our trials with a clear focus.

I had a dear pastor friend, Dr. Hugh Hall, who is now with the Lord. He used to say that he practiced looking through the Democrats and Republicans to see Christ. He reminded me of the perspective I must have as I journey through this fallen world. I must have eyes for Christ no matter what may be happening around me or who may be causing it.

Think about Jacob and Rachel. As you know in that story, Jacob served Laban for seven extra years to receive Rachel.

"So Jacob served seven years to get Rachel, but they seemed like only a few days to him because of his love for her" (Gen. 29:20).

It was hard work he expended, but it felt like only a few days because of his love for her. His perspective was formed by love so that the trial seemed like just a little thing. He was totally focused on the object of his love.

Many people have experienced this in the midst of trials. It is the relationships around us that often enable us to endure hard times. There is often a bonding that happens with others when going through hardship together.

Trials and Intimacy

Early in our marriage Sue and I faced a trial that brought us closer together. The doctor told us one of our little girls had leukemia and for many agonizing days we awaited further results.

Trials can create a tremendous intimacy.

Finally, the news came it was misdiagnosed and was actually a form of anemia. But during that time of trial we found a growing intimacy in our marriage relationship. Those moments have greatly strengthened us for other trials we have faced and may yet face.

Trials can create a tremendous intimacy. People have experienced this in athletics or the military, as they have gone through both joys and difficulties with those around them. They have played a tough game together or fought side by side in the heat of battle. There is a deep intimacy created, which is often hard to replicate apart from the experience of trials.

For the believer, the great thing about trials is that Christ goes through them with us. This experience results in an experience of deep intimacy with the Lord. Christ said:

"I will never leave you nor forsake you" (Heb. 13:5); "...And behold, I am with you always, to the end of the age." Matt. 28:20).

He is there, and his presence enables us to get through the trial, and even experience the sweetest joy. You will find that it is in the fire that your intimacy with Christ can become the greatest.

"He is always to be found in the thickest part of the battle. When the wind blows cold he always takes the bleak side of the hill. The heaviest end of the cross lies ever on his shoulders. If he bids us carry a burden, he carries it also. If there is anything that is gracious, generous, kind, and tender, yea lavish and superabundant in love, you always find it in him.... The vine holds nothing back from its branches, pouring all its life into them."[68]

Ask the three Hebrew young men who were thrown into the furnace of fire in Babylon. While in the fire, they found one like the son of God there with them (Dan. 3:24–25). Many believe this was the pre-incarnate Christ Himself.

It is possible to work hard for Christ, persevere through trials, to hate what God hates, and yet still lose our love for Christ.

This happened to the church of Ephesus, and it often happens to us as well. John's words hit home:

> *It is possible to work hard for Christ, persevere through trials, to hate what God hates, and yet still lose our love for Christ.*

"I know your works, your toil and your patient endurance, and how you cannot bear with those who are evil, but have tested those who call themselves apostles and are not, and found them to be false. I know you are enduring patiently and bearing up for my name's sake, and you have not grown weary. But I have this against you, that you have abandoned the love you had at first" (Rev. 2:2–4).

When you lose your love for Christ, trials don't feel like they last only a few days as it was with Jacob working for Rachel. They will seem to go on forever. We can go through trials without joy, because we are not focusing on our loving relationship with Christ. We have forgotten his gracious presence with us.

125

Are you lacking joy in the midst of your trial? Go back to your first love. This relationship will carry you through and give you joy. Recall the amazing truth that Christ has not abandoned you. He is with you.

Readjust Your Focus

Good stewardship in trials is a matter of re-adjusting our focus. My spiritual focus will determine how I navigate all of my trials—from the little bitty ones to the great "storm-rocking" ones. Peter knew what he was talking about. Now it is up to us to believe what he said and act on it.

Now comes the hard part—putting into practice what we have learned. There are three simple ways we can re-adjust our focus in trials.

First, we must not focus on the trial itself. Trials can be self-absorbing, blinding us to the sufficiency of God's Word and the comfort of God's presence in our lives. Focusing on the trial provides a distraction from the work God is doing. When the distraction is allowed to stay around, it increases our level of worry and anxiety and decreases our spiritual insight. Look to Christ and His promises while enduring the trial.

Second, look outside your trial to others who are suffering. The trial you are enduring is meant to sharpen your vision and give you better insight into the tribulations of others. It just may be the trial you have been given was sent for someone else's benefit. Being a servant of Christ means that we see our trials as a launching pad for greater service and blessing to others. We must not miss this stewardship opportunity.

Joseph experienced this very thing as he looked back on his trials. He testified:

"As for you, you meant evil against me, but God meant it for good, to bring it about that many people should be kept alive, as they are today"(Gen. 50:20).

Third, allow the trial to teach you something about the Lord Jesus you did not know before. Trials are lenses through which we can look at Jesus with renewed devotion and fall in worship at His feet with renewed wonder.. What He went through for us is absolutely astounding. The preoccupation of Jesus for the Father's will and His devotion to the mission of saving sinners draws us closer to Him as we suffer in our own valleys of pain. The trials of Jesus Christ yielded to God the greatest glory and to unworthy sinners the most amazing rescue ever heard of. Our trials must teach us of Jesus.

> *Trials are lenses through which we can look at Jesus with renewed devotion and fall in worship in worship at His feet with renewed wonder.*

Study Guide Questions

1. When we look ahead to the future God has promised, how does that view of tomorrow carry us through today with all its distractions and pains? What is it about the word of God and its promises that anchor us in the storms and give us direction in managing our trials as good stewards?

2. Abraham and Sarah endured many trials. Think about those trials: Leaving their home country to go to a place they did not know—enduring childlessness for many years, until it appeared that state would be final...the request to sacrifice their promised son on an altar. What carried them through these painful and often puzzling trials? Consider Hebrews 11:8–19. Where was their focus and what helped them maintain that focus? How did their focus affect their ability to manage their trials as good stewards?

3. Why are trials often necessary in our lives as believers? Consider Joseph's story in Genesis. Why do you think God brought Joseph into the valley of suffering as a young man? Notice how Joseph managed the trial of Potiphar's house recorded in Genesis 39. (The text seems to suggest good stewardship practice on the part of Joseph.) Where does Joseph seem to put his focus? Then look at his trial in Genesis 39–40 in the prison. Is there any good stewardship management principles you see here? Check out Joseph's conclusions as he looks back on his trials (see Gen. 50:19–21). What makes his understanding of his trials especially helpful for us in our own trials? Where was his focus at the end of his trials?

4. What are some things trials can protect us from? Make a list of those things and thank God for them.

5. How do trials equip us for more effective ministry? Can trials give us a stronger voice for God among our peers if we manage them well? In what way? How may our trials, for instance, advance the cause of the Gospel among our peers and family?

Chapter Five

Grace Work: Hannah's Stewardship of Her Trial
Text: 1 Samuel 1–2

A group of people were asked to write down some of the things that brought stress into their lives. Here are a few of their responses: "At the moment the most stressful things for me are dealing with my health issues, paying bills and feeling worthless because I can no longer do what I used to do...."

"I tend to worry over a matter. What if this happens or what if that happens, or how can I solve this? So I worry over problems— real or not real: the job status, money, my anger that comes at times."

"I take on things that I feel I can't handle. I don't know how to say 'no' and say, 'That's too much for me right now.' I stress over everything."

"It is very hard for me to not be able to please everyone. So this causes stress in my life."[69]

Trials are often the source of great stress. It is time to put a face on our trials. I want to show you a familiar Bible personality who could testify to the stress of her trial-yet she is one who managed her trial well as a good steward of God.

The Story behind Hannah's Story

Hannah's story is told in 1 Samuel 1–2. Here is what we need to know about this part of the Bible if we are to understand Hannah's story.

We are just coming out of the period of the Judges when 1 Samuel opens. In the book of Judges, you have no king; In 1 Samuel you have man's King (Saul); Later in 1 Samuel you finally have God's King (David).

The chief actor in this book is none other than God himself. The word *LORD* (*Yahweh*) is mentioned over sixty times in the first three chapters alone. You see men making all kinds of decisions in these chapters, but it is God who ultimately accomplishes His purposes. The Sovereignty of God dominates Hannah's story.

> "He governs the roll of dice (Prov. 16:33) and the rise of kings (Dan. 2:21). Nothing—from toothpicks to tyrants—is ultimately self-determining. Everything serves (willingly or not) the 'purpose of him who works all things according to the counsel of his will' (Eph. 1:11). God is the all-encompassing, all-pervading, all-governing reality."[70]

And we meet the boy Samuel who will be instrumental in God's accomplished purpose for Israel. Samuel's birth is a turning point in Israel's history. Through him God will once again reveal His Word to His people and give them victory over hostile enemies and establish a king who will lead the nation.

Remember that Samuel is not only the last Judge of Israel but the first of a new line of prophets after Moses (1 Sam. 3:19–21). He was a bridge-builder at a critical time in Jewish history when there was no strong earthly leader. His entrance on the scene of biblical history is the result of a direct intervention of God in human affairs because the text says that his mother could not have children.

1 Samuel 1:6 declares the reality of her situation: "Because the Lord had closed her womb."

Once again deliverance and salvation can only come from the Lord. Samuel's mother joins the elite company of ladies, like Sarah, Rebekah, Rachel, all of whom it is said the Lord had closed their wombs. So the theology driving our story is simply this: If deliverance comes—if Messiah comes—it will be by God's Sovereign hand, not by man's ability or resources.

Hannah's Story

Now let's get to Hannah's story. Her story teaches us that in severe trial, the grace of God works. In fact, Hannah's name actually means "grace." I have two granddaughters who have the middle name of grace. One is named Hanna Grace. (I call her "Grace Grace)." The other granddaughter is named Ellie Grace.

But grace does not look much like grace when we first meet Hannah. The beginning of Hannah's story is filled with tension in the household. It appears she is the first wife of Elkanah and because she is unable to provide him with children, he takes a second wife. That plan seems to meet with success because the second wife is able to have a lot of kids. But this unbiblical arrangement sows seeds of disaster in his home.

So Hannah's trial begins. She can't have children (and remember that God takes responsibility for that condition, the text tells us—1 Sam. 1:6). Perhaps Hannah even wonders if God is displeased with her in some way since she seems to be excluded from His promise of blessing (See Exod. 23:25–26). In the culture of that day to be unable to have children was devastating. A woman's value was measured by her fertility. What a bitter blow in Hannah's life.

The other wife relentlessly reminds her of her plight. Her husband does not understand her grief and her pastor is clueless about her trial. That's the picture now in front of us. Hannah's journey through trial will reveal to us some remarkable insights into trial management.

Trials Often Come from Those Closest to Us

Hannah learned that trials will often come to us from those closest to us. Hannah certainly experienced this sorrow. 1 Samuel 1:3–8 records the sad scenario of her life:

"Now this man used to go up year by year from his city to worship and to sacrifice to the LORD of hosts at Shiloh, where the two sons of Eli, Hophni and Phinehas, were priests of the LORD. On the day when Elkanah sacrificed, he would give portions to Peninnah his wife and to all her sons and daughters. But to Hannah he gave a double portion, because he loved her, though the LORD had closed her womb. And her rival used to provoke her grievously to irritate her, because the LORD had closed her womb. So it went on year by year. As often as she went up to the house of the LORD, she used to provoke her. Therefore Hannah wept and would not eat. And Elkanah, her husband, said to her, 'Hannah, why do you weep? And why do you not eat? And why is your heart sad? Am I not more to you than ten sons?'"

One Woman Man?

Meet Hannah's husband, Elkanah. He deepened her trial in two ways.

He deepened Hannah's trial through his disobedience. He disobeyed the Word of God. It does say in the text he loved his wife (1 Samuel 1:5 says, "He gave a double portion because he loved her.)" Now that's what a man should do. But there is a problem with this arrangement. He has two wives which is not according to God's will in marriage.

Learn this: Every time we depart from God's design for marriage we increase the effects of sin in the relationship. When you live with

> *Every time we depart from God's design for marriage we increase the effects of sin in the relationship.*

someone and are not married, you increase the effects of sin. When you choose a person of the same sex to live with in a sexual relationship and believe you can marry that individual, you increase the effects of sin. These relationships are in direct disobedience to God's Word (Lev. 18:22; Prov. 2:17; Matt. 19:4-6; Rom. 1:26-27;1 Cor. 5:1–13; 1 Thess. 4:3–8).

Elkanah should have known better because he was a Levite. We know this because he was a Kohathite from the family of Zuph who were Levites (1 Chron. 6:22–28, 34–35). Levites were scattered throughout the land of Israel and went to Shiloh to minister at the tabernacle whenever they were needed. Being a Levite he would be more familiar with God's law (the Word of God) than many of his countrymen. But he took two wives—against the teaching of God's Word—and as a result tension and conflict came to his home.

I asked my wife Sue if we lived in Bible times what she would think if I took another wife. She said, "You would still have only one wife, because either I go or she goes." And besides, what man in his right mind would want two wives living under the same roof. That's just plain dumb!!

Elkanah also deepened Hannah's trial by his insensitivity. Hannah must not only deal with a disobedient husband, but she also must deal with an insensitive husband. Disobedience blinds us to other things in life and here is an example of that. Elkanah shows little spiritual and emotional sensitivity to his wife's plight. He says several things to her that shows his lack of sensitivity to his wife and each statement just digs the hole deeper.

First he says, "Hannah, why are you crying?" Elkanah was saying something like this: "Come on don't pay attention to Peninnah, you know how she is."

Secondly he says, "And why do you not eat?" That's the same as saying "I'll take you out tonight, how's that?"

Then he says, "Why is your heart sad?" In other words, "Be happy."

Finally he says, "Am I not more to you than ten sons?" Now there is a truly insensitive man.. He in essence said, "Isn't it better to have me than a baby? You have me, what more could you want?" Wow. Can you believe this guy??

The Other Woman

But the trial deepens further with the invasion of Peninnah, the other wife. She further stirs the tension in the home with her barbed remarks. Her name means "coral" or "hard," and she lives up to her name. She seems jealous of Hannah because Elkanah shows preference for Hannah. Thus, she uses special occasions like going to worship to goad Hannah.

Year after year this baiting of Hannah goes on until Hannah breaks out in sobs. Dale Ralph Davis calls Peninnah

"...an overly fertile, mouthy, thorn in the flesh."[71]

Davis goes on to comment, however, that

> "We owe it to the God who takes even the smirks
> and digs and venom of Peninnahs and uses them to
> fill a cradle with another kingdom servant."[72]

Even in Hannah's worst trial, God is bringing something grand and powerful out of it all, but let's not get ahead of ourselves.

It gets even worse for Hannah. The trial hits rock bottom at church, in the very place you might expect comfort and encouragement. The spiritual leader of her church does not help lift the burden of her trial. In 1 Samuel 1:3 you have a very telling sentence: "Now this man used to go up year by year from his city to worship and to sacrifice to the LORD of hosts at Shiloh, where the two sons of Eli, Hophni and Phinehas, were priests of the LORD."

There is no guarantee that the people whom you depend on and count on the most will always be what you need.

Later we're told the true condition that existed in her church" "They [the sons of Eli] were worthless men, they did not know the Lord" (1 Samuel 2:12).

Eli the priest, when he saw her praying and weeping wrongly concluded that she was just another drunk and rebuked her.

So there you have it. Sometimes the trial comes from those closest to us as it did for Hannah. There is no guarantee that the people whom you depend on and count on the most will always be what you need. It was the Psalmist who confessed in Psalm 27:10: "For my father and my mother have forsaken me, but the LORD will take me in."

Trials Involving Our Children Are Often the Most Difficult

There is another insight worth noting. Trials involving our children are often the most difficult to face.

What we learn next from Hannah's story will strike a chord with many parents.

"After they had eaten and drunk in Shiloh, Hannah rose. Now Eli the priest was sitting on the seat beside the doorpost of the temple of the LORD. She was deeply distressed and prayed to the LORD and wept bitterly. And she vowed a vow and said, 'O LORD of hosts, if you will indeed look on the affliction of your servant and remember me and not forget your servant, but will give to your servant a son, then I will give him to the LORD all the days of his life, and no razor shall touch his head.' As she continued praying before the LORD, Eli observed her mouth. Hannah was speaking in her heart; only her lips moved, and her voice was not heard. Therefore Eli took her to be a drunken woman. And Eli said to her, 'How long will you go on being drunk? Put your wine away from you.' But Hannah answered, 'No, my lord, I am a woman troubled in spirit. I have drunk neither wine nor strong drink, but I have been pouring out my soul before the LORD. Do not regard your servant as a worthless woman, for all along I have been speaking out of my great anxiety and vexation'" (1 Sam. 1:9–16).

If we could have been there and listened to Hannah, not a person among us would be unmoved by her plea and her painful suffering. Children or the lack of children—both situations which involve children—can be a heavy burden.

Part of the task of a pastor is to encourage, advise, and admonish parents who weep and bear the burden of children who are in trouble. With an aching heart I have listened to many parents grieving over their children's circumstances.

It may be some physical trouble where a child faces a difficult operation. Sometimes, it may be mental, emotional, or spiritual trouble where a child rebels, heads into immorality or the drug world, and wanders away from Christ. At other times, it may include heartbroken couples who desire to have children but are unable to do so. Often, it involves grieving parents who lose a child in death. Maybe someone reading this can say, "Oh, yes, I certainly know what that's like." Hannah joins that heartbroken fellowship of women longing for children but unable to have them.

However, back then it was even worse than today, because in Jewish circles, not to bear children, especially sons, was viewed as a withdrawal of God's blessing from the life.

Notice the words in her prayer that reveal what is happening in her heart. In 1 Samuel 1:10 it says she is deeply distressed which means she is experiencing a severe type of depression and great emotional torment.

Here is a lady who is a believer yet she must deal with depression, and a lack of emotional well-being. She feels useless, overlooked, and at a loss.

Next, the text tells us she wept bitterly meaning just what you think it means. She cries bitter tears. She is hard pressed to see any good at this moment in her life. What reason does she have to continue going on? She cries out for God to look on her affliction (1 Sam. 1:11). She calls it affliction. This Hebrew word means misery. She has nowhere else to turn. Things at home with Peninnah were horrific in the face of unrelenting mockery. She found no comfort in her husband's inadequate sympathy and not even her pastor/priest understood her situation.

She goes on to speak of her great anxiety & vexation. As you can only imagine she is frustrated and filled with worry about what this condition will mean for her in the future if it is not alleviated (1 Sam. 1:16).

She describes herself as deeply troubled: "I am a woman troubled in spirit" (1 Sam. 1:15). She was so disturbed that she could no longer put it into words, but just move her mouth.

Eli misjudged her and thought she was drunk. Rest assured you will not always be understood by those you think should be understanding.

Trials Often Are Without Discernable Time Limits

Don't miss this insight from the text which may surprise you. Trials are often without discernable time limits.

It is always tough when you have to wait. 1 Samuel 1:17–20 records the following: "Then Eli answered, 'Go in peace and the God of Israel grant your petition that you have made to him.' And she said, 'Let your servant find favor in your eyes.' Then the woman went her way and ate, and her face was no longer sad. They rose early in the morning and worshiped before the LORD; then they went back to their house at Ramah. And Elkanah knew Hannah his wife, and the LORD remembered her. And in due time Hannah conceived and bore a son, and she called his name Samuel, for she said, 'I have asked for him from the LORD.'"

The text continues to inform us of the outcome of that prayer meeting (1 Samuel 2:20–21): "Then Eli would bless Elkanah and his wife, and say, 'May the LORD give you children by this woman for the petition she asked of the LORD.' So then they would return to their home. Indeed the LORD visited Hannah, and she conceived and bore three sons and two daughters. And the young man Samuel grew in the presence of the LORD."

Even when she discovered through Eli that God was going to answer her prayer, she still did not know when it would happen. She seems to have the confidence that only sheer trust in the living God can bring to you when you have to wait on the answer. She went back no longer sad (1 Sam. 1:18).

I find what she does next absolutely remarkable. She participates in worship the next morning before the Lord with that rag-tag family of hers.

> *When you are waiting by faith on God to act, you can move forward in joyful worship, regardless of what circumstances have not immediately changed in your life, because you are confident God will act.*

Tuck this lesson away. When you are waiting by faith on God to act, you can move forward in joyful worship, regardless of what circumstances have not immediately changed in your life, because you are confident God will act. This does not mean that you will get want you asked for, but it does mean that you will receive what a good God chooses to give you. And what God gives you is good because He is good.

Let's jump ahead for a moment, because there is a beautiful outcome.

The text says "in due time" Hannah conceived. Like a blinking light in the text the trial comes to a close.

There is a wonderful after-time line here. Yes, she gives up her son. Does she continue in the faith after giving up her son? Does she continue childless, since her boy is gone from her? Does her little boy Samuel make it?

We find the answer to these questions in 1 Samuel 2:18–21: "Samuel was ministering before the LORD, a boy clothed with a linen ephod. And his mother used to make for him a little robe and take it to him each year when she went up with her husband to offer the yearly sacrifice. Then Eli would bless Elkanah and his wife, and say, 'May the LORD give you children by this woman for the petition she asked of the LORD.' So then they would return to their home. Indeed the LORD visited Hannah, and she conceived and bore three sons and two daughters. And the young man Samuel grew in the presence of the LORD.'"

Trials Bring out the Reality of Our Faith

Going back and picking up our story-line we notice yet another significant insight in Hannah's story which hits us like a hammer. Trials bring out the reality of our faith when we pray. And prayer is absolutely essential to the reality of our faith. For Hannah, prayer was the first and last resort in her trial. Notice 1 Samuel 1:9–18:

"After they had eaten and drunk in Shiloh, Hannah rose. Now Eli the priest was sitting on the seat beside the doorpost of the temple of the LORD. She was deeply distressed and prayed to the LORD and wept bitterly. And she vowed a vow and said, 'O LORD of hosts, if you will indeed look on the affliction of your servant and remember me and not forget your servant, but will give to your servant a son, then I will give him to the LORD all the days of his life, and no razor shall touch his head.' As she continued praying before the LORD, Eli observed her mouth. Hannah was speaking in her heart; only her lips moved, and her voice was not heard. Therefore Eli took her to be a drunken woman. And Eli said to her, 'How long will you go on being drunk? Put your wine away from you.' But Hannah answered, 'No, my lord, I am a woman troubled in spirit. I have drunk neither wine nor strong drink, but I have been pouring out my soul before the LORD. Do not regard your servant as a worthless woman, for all along I have been speaking out of my great anxiety and vexation.' Then Eli answered, 'Go in peace, and the God of Israel grant your petition that you have made to him.' And she said, 'Let your servant find favor in your eyes.' Then the woman went her way and ate, and her face was no longer sad.'"

Her first prayer is quite remarkable. It reveals a robust and renewed faith. Five times she calls herself "your servant" (three times in 1:11; one time in 1:16; and one time in 1:18). She submits to God in her prayer. She addresses him as "Lord of Hosts." She believes that God will not forget her because He is the sovereign God of all the hosts, or literally "the armies." This is the God who has the total resources of the universe at his disposal. What an understanding of sovereign omnipotence.

She seems to believe that God will notice the broken heart of a relatively obscure woman in the hill country of Ephraim and that her broken heart really matters to him. If God can see and hear the affliction of his people in the days of Moses (see Exod. 3:7) then surely He could see and hear the distress of an individual servant.

She also does not ask that her son become famous or prominent. All that matters is that he will belong to Yahweh (1:11). She kept praying and poured out her soul as she prayed (1:15b).

When you step back from her life for a moment and look at the total picture, you see that grace, gratitude, and integrity marked the outcome of her trial. 1 Samuel 1:24–28 says it all:

"And when she had weaned him, she took him up with her, along with a three-year-old bull, an ephah of flour, and a skin of wine, and she brought him to the house of the LORD at Shiloh. And the child was young. Then they slaughtered the bull, and they brought the child to Eli. And she said, 'Oh, my lord. As you live, my lord, I am the woman who was standing here in your presence, praying to the LORD. For this child I prayed, and the LORD has granted me my petition that I made to him. Therefore I have lent him to the LORD. As long as he lives, he is lent to the LORD.' And he worshiped the LORD there.'"

She follows through on her vow to God regarding Samuel. This could not have been easy knowing the atmosphere that existed in Shiloh with the godless sons of Eli and the weak, tolerant attitude of Eli their father-priest. Wouldn't she have worried about little Samuel coming under such an influence? What a risk. But she trusted it all to the will of God.

Just a side note for us to think about. Hannah had to have told Elkanah about her vow because Jewish law permits a husband to annul a wife's vow if he disagreed with it (see Num. 30). She could not have followed through with her vow in secret.

Ladies, be encouraged about the change God can make in a disobedient, insensitive husband (or for that matter any people obstacle you might face). It appears Elkanah agreed with her decision and allowed her to remain at home with her son when the rest of the family went on its annual trip to Shiloh. He gave his permission to fulfill the vow. Think of what this would have meant. His first born son of the wife he loves is the object of this decision and he gives him up (Doesn't this remind us of the Gospel where God gave up His Son for others?). Don't forget that a firstborn son had to be redeemed by a sacrifice under Jewish law, but here Elkanah actually gives up his son.

When What You Ask for Comes

Hannah testifies to Eli on the day of presentation that she was the woman who three years before asked for a son and God answered. She speaks several times in 1 Samuel 1:27–28 using the word *ask*. Here is how it reads literally: "For this child I prayed, and Yahweh gave me my asking which I asked from him; and I also have given back what was asked to Yahweh; all the days he lives he is one that is asked for Yahweh."

Samuel's name thus means "asked of God" and "heard of God." The name is in three parts: Sa-al, meaning "asked," and sama meaning "heard," coupled with "el" meaning "God."

Warren Wiersbe wisely commented on this scene:

> "All his life, Samuel was both an answer to prayer
> and a great man of prayer."[73]

Her last prayer is also amazing for it confesses faith in the sovereign goodness of God as the key to surviving her trial.

"And Hannah prayed and said, 'My heart exults in the LORD; my strength is exalted in the LORD. My mouth derides my enemies, because I rejoice in your salvation. There is none holy like the LORD; there is none besides you; there is no rock like our God. Talk no more so very proudly, let not arrogance come from your mouth; for the LORD is a God of knowledge, and by him actions are weighed. The bows of the mighty are broken, but the feeble bind on strength. Those who were full have hired themselves out for bread, but those who were hungry have ceased to hunger. The barren has borne seven, but she who has many children is forlorn. The LORD kills and brings to life; he brings down to Sheol and raises up. The LORD makes poor and makes rich; he brings low and he exalts. He raises up the poor from the dust; he lifts the needy from the ash heap to make them sit with princes and inherit a seat of honor. For the pillars of the earth are the LORD's, and on them he has set the world. 'He will guard the feet of his faithful ones, but the wicked shall be cut off in darkness, for not by might shall a man prevail. The adversaries of the LORD shall be broken to pieces; against them he will thunder in heaven. The LORD will judge the ends of the earth; he will give strength to his king and exalt the power of his anointed.' Then Elkanah went home to Ramah. And the boy ministered to the LORD in the presence of Eli the priest" (1 Sam. 2:1–10).

What God taught Hannah in her trial is worth our attention (2:1–3). God is now personal to her. Notice the use of those little words *my* and *I*. God is now exclusive in her theology. And because God is now sovereign in her thinking, she no longer fears any action of man toward her.

What God did for her and through her is encouraging to us in our trials as well (read 2:4–8 again). God took her weakness and need and made it a platform for showing His strength. Remember He did the same with the Apostle Paul (2 Cor. 12:7–10).

> *God took her weakness and need and made it a platform for showing His strength.*

God also reverses her afflictions. That's the way God rules. As you go through the Old Testament you cannot help but notice all the "reversals" God brings in the circumstances of his people. His plan always succeeds because He is a Sovereign God who is wise in the reversals of grace that He bestows.

But there is more. Notice in 1 Samuel 2:9–10 that God guards his faithful servants, defeats their enemies, and strengthens and secures his godly leaders as they serve his people

At the worst of times God provides needed leadership for his people. That's why we need to remember that there is always a bigger purpose being worked out through my trial than I can see at the moment. Back in Genesis we read where the Patriarch Joseph realized God's greater purpose in trial by placing him in a vital leadership position through the betrayal of his brothers, the false accusation in Potiphar's house, and the forgotten request in prison (Gen. 50:18-20). Hannah also came to realize that God had a grand purpose for her and her son and that put her trial into perspective.

Prayer as a Means God Uses

God often uses prayer as a means of our deliverance from trials. Who can forget Peter's release from prison through the prayers of the church (Acts 12), and Paul and Silas being released from the Philippian jail after their mid-night prayers (Acts 16).

Hannah prayed, God heard, and a nation was impacted through the son she asked for.

Prayer also eases the stress of our troubles because it is God's vehicle for laying our burdens on Him. The book of Psalms is full of the prayers of God's suffering saints. William Bradbury's old hymn Sweet Hour of Prayer speaks to the interaction of our prayers and trials:

> Sweet hour of prayer, sweet hour of prayer,
> That calls me from a world of care
> And bids me at my Father's throne
> Make all my wants and wishes known.
> In seasons of distress and grief
> My soul has often found relief
> And oft escaped the tempter's snare
> By thy return, sweet hour of prayer.[74]

Prayer was instrumental in protecting and sustaining Hannah in the midst of her trial. Her trial is a great reminder to us that God is just and that even though we may not know the reason for our trial, our compassionate and gracious God puts a light at the end of the tunnel for those who trust Him and who seek His face.. It does not always mean we get what we ask for, but it does mean God gives what we need most. That's how grace works.

Keep this truth in front of you during your own trials. Grace works. Ask Hannah. She will tell you.

As we conclude our little journey with Hannah, we are reminded that it is not uncommon to feel the stress that comes with a deep and heavy trial. It may be a severe illness, or an unresolved marital problem, or an overwhelming financial burden that weighs you down. We are also reminded that it is not uncommon for us to experience the failures of people we counted on for support in trial.

In these moments, there are two steps we can take to avail ourselves of God's amazing grace.

Step One: Believe that God has provided prayer as a stress reliever for us in trial. Hannah found the recourse to prayer a stabilizing factor in her life during her suffering. The stress diminishes as she engages in fervent prayer. The outcome of her prayer was a wonderful experience of God's grace. The writer of Hebrews tells us that the throne of grace is where we find mercy and find grace to help in time of need (Heb. 4:16). Try writing out your prayers as a means of concentrating on what you want to tell the Lord. Put it in an envelope and tuck it in a box and call it your trial box. This will remind you that our prayers are stored up before God. After all, we are told that the prayers of the saints are a sweet fragrance to the Lord (Rev. 5:8).

Step Two: Don't expect too much from people when you are in the midst of suffering. All of us have weaknesses in the flesh and to over-expect from people will often put us in a downward spiral. The Lord Himself declares that He is the only reliable rock upon which we can rest (Isa. 26:4; 44:8). The old hymn by George Duffield entitled Stand up, Stand up for Jesus puts it well:

> Stand up. stand up for Jesus.
> Stand in His strength alone;
> The arm of flesh will fail you;
> Ye dare not trust your own.
> Put on the Gospel armor,
> And, watching unto prayer,
> Where duty calls, or danger,
> Be never wanting there.

Jeremiah 17:5–10 calls us away from the flesh as a means of support:

"Thus says the LORD: Cursed is the man who trusts in man and makes flesh his strength, whose heart turns away from the LORD. He is like a shrub in the desert, and shall not see any good come. He shall dwell in the parched places of the wilderness, in an uninhabited salt land. Blessed is the man who trusts in the LORD, whose trust in the LORD. He is like a tree planted by water, that sends out its roots by the stream, and does not fear when heat comes, for its leaves remain green, and is not anxious in the year of drought, for it does not cease to bear fruit. The heart is deceitful above all things, and desperately sick, who can understand it. I the LORD search the heart and test the mind...."

Study Guide Questions

1. Hagar, Sarah's maid certainly faced some major trials. Did she bring them on herself? Part of that may be debatable. Read Genesis 16. In what way do you see God's grace at work in her trials? What is significant about her statements in 16:13? ("You are a God of seeing.... Truly here I have seen him who looks after me.") How strong should the reality of God's grace factor into my trial experiences? In what way does God's grace help me manage my trials as a good steward?

2. How does a trial bring out the reality of your faith? What evidence do we have that God is trustworthy in the midst of suffering? From Scripture? From personal history?

3. Think of the many women in the Bible who were barren until God opened their wombs. There was Sarah, Rebekah, Rachael, Manoah's wife, and of course Hannah and Elizabeth (Zechariah's wife), etc. We witness God opening the wombs of those women in sovereign grace to fulfill his redemptive plan for sinful men. But many women never get that kind of ending to their trial. How does God bring comfort to those of His children to whom, in His sovereign wisdom, He says no? Is it possible God has a better plan for them? (See Hebrews 11:36–40. Note that not all received a reward for their faith in this life).

4. Hannah emerges from this trial with a godly perspective still intact. What was Hannah's greatest concern for her son Samuel? (Look at I Sam. 1:11, 22, 26–28.) How does her concern show good stewardship management of her trial? What can emerge from our trials that will have great value for our children and grandchildren?

5. Examine Hannah's remarkable prayer in I Samuel 2:1–10. Notice the strong theology in Hannah's prayer. What is Hannah's view of God that seems to have held her sanity intact through all she suffered? Where do you see grace and faith at work in the words of her prayer? Could this be the key to our own stewardship management of our suffering?

Chapter Six

Patient Work:
Job's Stewardship of His Trial
Text: Job 1–2

Y our life, as a follower of Jesus Christ, is all about displaying
the superiority of a life lived in Christ. Christians get cancer,
have sorrows, and set-backs as well. But, the sons and daughters of
the Lord handle things differently than the sons and daughters of
this world.

The Question That Hits Hardest

There are some stories that really stick with you. I remember
a true story Chuck Swindoll told on one of his broadcasts several
years ago about a young man named Glen Chambers. Glen had a
heart to serve God on the mission field. He got his training, went to
Bible college, went on to seminary, and then raised his support for
missionary service. He left everything behind and boarded a plane
to fly as a missionary to South America. He had gone through the
strain of financial problems and misunderstanding with his family.
He'd dealt with the pain of separation, and he was filled with hope

and anticipation and excitement about serving Christ. As he was about to fly, he thought to himself, I really should have said more to my parents, so he tore off a corner of a magazine he found at the airport and wrote them a little note: "Mom and Dad, I'm so excited, going to serve Christ. Thanks for getting behind me in this. I love you, Glen." Glen stuffed the note in an envelope and put it in the mail to his parents.

Glen got on the plane, and in the middle of the night, a mountain in the jungles of Ecuador reached up, pulled that plane out of the sky, and Glen was killed in a plane crash. He never made it. All the training, all the fundraising—everything—and he never got there.

After the funeral was over, his parents got the letter Glen wrote. They opened it. It turns out that on the back of the magazine corner he'd torn off to write that note was printed one word: "Why?"

As Swindoll told the story, he went on to say that this is the question that hits the hardest; it's the question that hurts the most; it's the question that lingers the longest; it's the question that every follower of Jesus Christ has asked. You've asked it. "Why, God?"

If anyone could raise that question and advise us on its answer, it is probably the man Job in the Bible. I don't think we could leave this subject without taking a look at Job. His trials are very well known and he was one of the few men of history who managed his trials well as a good steward of God.

Just Plain Wrong

Historically, people have wrongly held two beliefs about God when they have experienced suffering and trial in this life.

One belief states that God is good and is helpless to stem the evil and trouble that comes into human life. There is a limit on his ability to control evil events. He is not almighty. Years ago, Rabbi

Harold Kushner wrote a book advocating this view entitled *When Bad Things Happen to Good People*. This book was prompted by the fact that his three-year-old son was diagnosed with a degenerative disease. The doctors informed him that his son would only live until his early teens. Thus, he took comfort in the fact God could not do anything about it.

Yet this wrongly held belief about God runs in total contradiction to the God we see in the Bible. God is not helpless. God is sovereign in the affairs of life down here.

The second belief states that God is not good and therefore caused or allowed those troubles. The thinking goes like this: If I had the power of God, I would stop such things from happening. As a result of this kind of thinking some have lost faith in the goodness of God. This belief also contradicts the picture of God we are given in the Scriptures. God is consistently shown as good and holy and yes, just.

As we turn to the book of Job for answers, we can argue against both of those positions decisively.

Trials Are Not Academic

Christopher Ash sets the tone for understanding the book of Job:

> "This book is not merely academic: it is both about and for people who know suffering. Job is a fireball book. It is a staggeringly honest book. It is a book that knows what people actually say and think—and not just what they say publicly in church. It knows what people say behind closed doors and in whispers; and it knows what we say in our tears."[75]

The introduction to the book of Job portrays a scene in which the right people come out on top. A godly man is ruling his home well. A successful businessman is living with integrity. And a household is prospering under godly leadership. After reading the introduction to the book of Job we could go home happy. But then the action begins.

In the first two chapters you have four alternating scenes—two in heaven and two on earth. What you see is a great, godly man who continues to be a godly man when he ceases to be a great man. He is beset with innumerable, unthinkable trials such as rarely happens to a human being and yet, he emerges intact, still walking on in his faith. The scene in heaven reveals what set all those trials in motion.

In the heavenly scenes the question arises (brought on, by the way, as an accusation by Satan before God) as to whether a man is godly just because he is prosperous and has been dealt a good life. Or is it possible that his blessings of prosperity had nothing to do with his being godly? The question is answered for us when the man's prosperity and good life are removed, and he still continues to be godly. Job is the subject of this "experiment" in suffering.

If anyone can teach us how to manage our trials as good stewards, it certainly is this man. We are going to examine what Job learned that helped him manage his trials as a good steward of God. It is no wonder we are called on to think of Job as a patient man. He waited on God and did not give in to sin.

Lessons When under Fire

There are five basic lessons that come to the surface in our text about a man under the fire of extreme trials.

Lesson #1: Committed believers do not get a pass on trials: Trials DO come to people who know & love the Lord (Job 1:1–5)

Remember that Job from all we know was not a Jew (1:1). He lived in the land of Uz which was possibly in Edom. The importance of the land of Uz in this context is not in where it was but in where it was not. It was not in Israel. Job lived outside the promised land. His story does not tie in to any known events in Israel's history. His story does not begin "in the somethingth year" of so-and-so, king of Israel or Judah or at any identifiable time in Israel's history. In fact, notice in 1:5 that Job offers sacrifices on behalf of his family in a way that would have been strictly forbidden after the institution of the Jewish priesthood.

Furthermore, he seems to have been a contemporary of Abraham, Isaac, or Jacob. If we understand the time of the writing of his book (which is considered to be one of the oldest pieces of biblical literature) he would have lived independently of the giving of the promises to Abraham and before the captivity in and exodus from Egypt. He also would have lived before the giving of the law at Mount Sinai and before the conquest of the Promised Land.

This makes his story incredible for here is a man who knows the one true God apart from Israel. His name has a two-fold meaning: "One who weeps" and "One ever returning to God." So Job emerges from the introduction to his book as a godly believer, an exemplary family man, and a successful business man.

But above all, Job emerges as a man who knows & fears God (1:1–9; 2:3). The text tells us that he is blameless in his character (see 1:1). This word means "genuine and authentic." Joshua exhorts the people of Israel to serve God "in sincerity" (same Hebrew word— Joshua 24:14). Literally, the Hebrew word can be translated "genuinely," which means not just pretending to serve Him while their hearts were somewhere else but in authentic sincerity.

Jotham challenges the people of Shechem with these words: "Now therefore if you acted in good faith and integrity when you made Abimelech King...." (Judg. 9:16). (The same Hebrew word—i.e. if you meant what you said and were not trying to deceive or double-cross anyone)

In Genesis 17:1, God said to Abraham, "Walk before me, and be blameless."

There is the word again. Psalm 119:1 proclaims a blessing on the one whose way is blameless. This is another way of saying, "What you see is what you get."

When you saw Job at work, when you heard his words, when you watched his deeds, you were seeing an accurate reflection of what was going on in his heart.

So the word means personal integrity not sinless perfection. When you saw Job at work, when you heard his words, when you watched his deeds, you were seeing an accurate reflection of what was going on in his heart. Job was not hiding anything. He was not a hypocrite. He lived what he said he believed.

Then the text tells us that he is upright in his dealings (1:1). This is a word that refers to the way we treat other people. In his human relationships he is straightforward, a man you can do business with because he will not double-cross you or cheat you.

Next we learn that he is a God-fearer in his spiritual life (1:1). He had a reverence and respect for God. I like Charles Bridges definition of fearing God: "That affectionate reverence, by which the child of God bends himself humbly and carefully to his Father's law."[76]

Job was what we would call a genuinely godly man.

Perhaps this comes out in the strongest way when we look ahead to Job 1:5–6 and notice how consistently he prays for and leads his children in spiritual matters. They all got together for the kids' birthdays and had a party. They seemed to be a happy family, yet Job had some concerns.

When each party came to an end, Job summoned all of his children for a ceremony of sacrifice. The text tells us he would rise early in the morning and offer sacrifices for each one of them.

Later in Israel's history a burnt offering would be the most expensive form of sacrifice, in which the whole sacrificial animal is consumed. This was to picture God's anger in burning up the animal in the place of the worshipper. I can imagine Job saying something like this: "This animal is for you," and he lights the fire and the animal is consumed. As each son or daughter would watch this they could not help but think that's what would have happened to me if there had not been a sacrifice. Job was a deeply concerned father about the spiritual welfare of his children. Though his kids outwardly seemed godly, he knew the human heart well and that appearances can be deceiving. This is the early shadow cast over what seems to be a happy scene. The words of an old puritan writer come to mind:

> "Ah, the sinful human heart always lurks to break
> out in rebellion against God"[77]

Proverbs 14:26 tells us that "In the fear of the LORD one has strong confidence, and his children will have a refuge."

Don't miss the instructive little foot note to all of this: Thus did Job continually (Job 1:5).

What a challenge to us as fathers and even grandfathers. Our children and grandchildren cry out for a consistent, godly pattern to be set in front of them where our faith is lived out and not just lectured.

God also makes a point of telling us that Job is moral in his everyday life. In other words he was known for righteous living.

"Who turned away from evil" (Job 1:1).

Now to turn away from evil has the idea of repenting. It is not that Job never sinned or made mistakes. He certainly did. In fact Job admits to this very thing when he speaks of "the iniquities of my youth" in Job 13:26 and "my sin" in Job 14:16 and later confesses in dust and ashes (Job 42:5–6).

This was a habitual practice for him. He cultivated the practice of turning away from evil as a regular routine of life. Job is included in the book of Ezekiel with such men as Noah and Daniel as a man of conspicuous righteousness (Ezek. 14:14). We are told in the text that these men were righteous "by faith."

> *You will notice that events in a believer's life on earth have their source in heaven.*

No sinner has ever been righteous before God in any other way.

So here is the picture that emerges of Job. He is successful and blessed in his business life. He has camels (3000)—like a fleet of trucks today. He has donkeys. Think of a garage full of cars. He has a lot of sheep—a large ranch.

But don't just think of his blessings as consisting of material ones alone. He is also blessed in his personal life. He has seven sons, and three daughters. In that time in history, having a lot of children marked you as one who had the favor of the gods.

Even more remarkable we find Job to be a spiritual man who placed God at the forefront of his life and business.

Now we are ready for lesson two.

Lesson #2: God sets and measures every one of our trials: Every trial, no matter its source, comes to us through God's hands (Job 1:6–12).

Listen to these instructive words:

There was a day (Job 1:6).

Again there was a day (Job 2:1).

Something happened in heaven that would change Job's life on earth forever. You will notice that events in a believer's life on earth have their source in heaven.

Here others are introduced into the narrative, namely, God and Satan. God is seen in the beginning and ending of the book while Satan is only seen in the beginning.

> "Scripture never puts Satan and his activities front and center. God puts people and our relationship to him and each other front and center. Then, just often enough, so you don't forget, he lifts the curtain and says, 'By the way—'and gives you a glimpse of what's happening backstage."[78]

There is a meeting, a required meeting it appears, of accountability before God for all the angelic beings God created. Notice some significant, descriptive words here. The phrase "sons of God" speaks of beings whose existence is derived from God (hence sons) but whose rank is superhuman (see Ps. 29:1; Ps. 82 and 89).

The phrase "to present themselves" means to attend a meeting to which you have been summoned. The word *Satan* literally means "adversary, opponent, enemy."

An accounting is then asked for. Now God's questions and Satan's answers reveal to us something very telling about our enemy. It appears that the last thing Satan wanted to do was come to that meeting and give an accounting and especially have his doings go on public record. This question and answer session between God and Satan is an expose' of Satan's strategy. The conversation went something like this:

God: So what have you been up to and where have you been?

Satan: Oh, I have been here and there doing this and that.

(Don't miss the vagueness of his response. God is going to force him to come out in the open.)

God: Have you considered Job my servant and what he is like? (You had better believe he had, and God knew it.)

God uses the term "my servant" to describe Job. This phrase "my servant" is used 40 times of Moses. It is a title of dignity, honor, friendship, and relationship. It is also used to describe God's prophets and the patriarchs. He is my servant...What a declaration. Could God say that of us?

Job is loyal to God and so God addresses him as "my servant." And we will discover that God is loyal to his servants.

Satan continues the conversation by raising the million-dollar question:

Satan: Well, the only reason anyone would serve you so devotedly is because of how you bless them. Why wouldn't Job be all goody-two-shoes. You've given him everything.

So the question comes then: Are we godly for our own benefit or for God's benefit?

Satan believed the prosperity gospel. He originated it. Remember his conversation with Eve in Genesis 3? If you take the fruit, you get all this stuff. That's where the prosperity gospel came from. If you live a life of godliness, then you get rich.

Don't miss this. Satan is probing: He asks: Why is Job really godly? His conclusion? Because he gets good stuff in life for being like that. Who wouldn't?

The Satan speech continues. Next, he says two very significant and revealing things:

> *Satan cannot move against us unless God moves his hand and allows it.*

1: Satan says: Have you not put a hedge around him, and his house, and all he has? (Job 1:9). This is a very profound and revealing confession. Satan had tested the boundaries and discovered

this reality. God protects his own; God secures his own; God has fences around his own. Isn't this fact astounding and comforting to us when we are in the middle of some painful and stretching trial?

2: Satan says: Stretch out your hand and touch. (Job 1:11)

This statement is also very significant because it reveals that Satan can do nothing to Job. God has to move his hand for Job to be touched by any kind of adversity and Satan knows it. So here is the bottom line to all of this. Satan cannot move against us unless God moves his hand and allows it. God moves his hand and says to Satan that he can only go so far and no further.

God: OK you can touch his family, his stuff, but you cannot touch him.

And we know what happens next. The trial comes blasting in on Job with full force.

Now catch your breath here. Listen, the fact is this: God measures the type of trials we have (all that he has is in your hands). God also sets the limits of the trials we face (only don't touch him). The maximums and the minimums of our trials are all measured and limited by the hand of our Friend, our Lord, and our God. All you have to do is notice how many names God's hand is referred to in this conversation in the text.

David Powilson in his book *Seeing with New Eyes* comments on the Sovereign hand of God at work in our lives:

> "God says, in effect, 'People of God it all makes sense. It's all working out according to a definite plan. A hand is on the controls of history and of your life, with the power to perform what he chooses.... His will of control (Eph. 1:11) is to be trusted as the frame of reference behind every experience....' The supremacy of God's purposes is not a debating point. It is the foundation of indestructible confidence

and ravishing delight. God is in control, and you
can bend all your energies to your calling, trusting
that God's plans are working out.... God's chief purpose is to take us up to the highest lookout point.
We are in the hands of a Man with a plan."[79]

David had experience with God's hand too. David was right
when he confessed:

"My times are in Your hands" (Ps. 31:15).

Many believe that this psalm was written during the period of
Saul's pursuit of David in the wilderness. David learned firsthand
what it means to be in the hand of God.

Make a note of this. God is not afraid to go on record as being
responsible for what came into Job's life. The trials came through the
hands of a friend. What a blessing to know. But here is the question:
Does Job know this? The answer is absolutely. Job confesses that he
knows it is God's hand that has touched him.

"Have mercy on me, have mercy on me, O you my friends, for
the hand of God has touched me. Why do you, like God, pursue
me? Why are you not satisfied with my flesh?" (Job 19:21–22).

Our next stewardship lesson from Job, however, takes us into
some rough waters.

Lesson #3: There is no such thing as an "easy" trial: Trials are
very hard but worship is always possible (Job 1:13–22).

Look at all the losses Job now suffers. He must contend with the
loss of his business, his securities, his assets, and if that's not enough,
he must face the grief of losing his children—all of them in one fell
swoop. In a short period of time, Job went into the deepest valley
of trial any human being could possibly experience. Job's trials are
recorded in a way that lets us feel the onslaught of each one.

But the plot thickens. Job feels like God is against him. It seems
to Job that God has attacked him, shooting his arrows into him (Job

6:4), and that God has isolated him from just about everyone in his life (Job 19:13–19).

> "Here are all the armies of the Lord of hosts advancing in force, preparing to lay siege. And to what great city are they laying siege? 'Just little me, little old Job in my one-man tent.' It is as if one of us goes for a night's camping on our own. We wake, peep out of the tent and all around us are tanks and gun emplacements; overhead is the entire United States Air Force. All bent on attacking me...And then, not only has God attacked him. He has made sure Job is completely alone when attacked. There is no one else in the tent."[80]

My friend, there are no easy trials. But the story goes on.

Notice the repeat of that phrase: "Now there was a day...." (Job 1:13).

The scene now shifts from heaven to earth.

It is the birthday of the oldest son and the kids are all gathered there. For some reason that we do not know, Job is not there yet at the party. He is interrupted and told that his business has come under attack. The terrorists of the day had struck. The protective hedge had been moved (not removed, mind you; there is a difference). The world that he thought was safe, was not. One servant after another comes, reporting multiple disasters. Finally, the worst news of all comes. It appears that a tornado struck the house where the kids were gathered, and they all lost their lives. None survived.

We cannot imagine such horror. The losses are overwhelming. The family business is gone, Job is bankrupt, wiped out, poverty stricken and now he has ten funerals to plan. All the kids are gone. Imagine what torture the holidays would be for this man.

So the real test sets in. How will Job respond? Does he serve God for what God gives him or does Job serve God because God is worthy of his worship? How do you manage all of that?

As if all of these trials are not enough, more is on the horizon for Job.

Lesson #4: Trials often come in pairs: One trial is often followed closely by another trial but God is still there (Job 2:1–10).

God is not showing off to Satan by continuing the trial in Job's life. Stephen Kaung, in his book *The Splendor of His Ways* says:

> "No, it was not a matter of God's showing off, for He does not enjoy seeing His people suffer. It was because He had a definite purpose in mind concerning Job. God knew His servant and knew precisely what He was doing."[81]

The Bible comforts us on this point. "Behold, we consider those blessed who remained steadfast. You have heard of the steadfastness of Job, and you have seen the purpose of the Lord, how the Lord is compassionate and merciful" (James 5:11).

Now we have a repeat of the former meeting in heaven. Here is this regular accounting session again. The same subject comes up.

Job's trials are not over. After all of that, God allows Satan to touch his body, but he cannot take his life. Job's body becomes diseased. This trial affects his personal health. We are meant to be shocked, because chapter one ends as if his trials are all over. Watch the matter Satan now brings up before God about Job.

Satan: Yeah, OK, He handled that. What a person has is one thing, but what a person is, now that is another thing.

We would have expected God to say enough is enough. The man has suffered enough, and his godliness and loyalty are well-proven. End of trial. Case closed. That's what we would have concluded.

But the Lord disagrees with us and that unexpected action of God teaches us something very profound. The agents of our trials change. In the first set of trials, human and impersonal agents inflict tragedy (Sabeans, Chaldeans, lightning and a tornado). Here the enemy, Satan, makes it personal. He is permitted to bring this trial himself. So once again the hedge is moved (not removed, mind you, but moved) and Job is covered in sores that are unrelentingly painful. There seems to be no cure. He sits in the ashes (Job 2:8) where the garbage is burned in a heap outside the city gate each day. What we see is such a totally pathetic picture. Job is not in a hospital bed with clean sheets, but in the ashes of a garbage dump with a broken piece of pottery with which to scratch himself. (Job 2:8).

Now at this point in Job's story you would think that finally, this is the end of his trials. But you would be wrong.

Buckle up, for yet another trial appears on the horizon in the form of his beloved wife. Job's wife becomes disheartened. Mrs. Job makes her only appearance in the drama here. All we know is this: At some moment of lonely suffering she pleads with Job to curse God. Remarkably, Job and Mrs. Job do not divorce. They did not divorce. Later they have many more children, so they stayed together against overwhelming odds. Job and his wife could do some major and much needed marriage counseling today for many of our married couples.

Don't be too hard on Mrs. Job. She has had enough of suffering. Seeing her husband wasting away she opts out. She knows, as Job knows, that to curse God ultimately brings a human being under the sentence of death. She put a terrible temptation in front of Job. Let it go, give it up, it is just not worth it. She had no explanation. But she appears to offer a solution, though not a good and righteous one.

A. W. Tozer in his book *The Knowledge of the Holy* warns us that in the midst of trials it is easy to consider our faith no more than an insurance policy.[82] Job's faith was rock solid in the Lord, unlike insurance policies which are only as good as the company that backs them. He confesses that receiving good or evil does not change his mind about his faithfulness to God.

> "Under the pressure of sore affliction men are in danger of falling into one or other of two opposite extremes, either of which is inconsistent with fidelity to the Lord's service. The first is that of repining and murmuring at the divine allotment: The other is that of bearing it in a spirit of stoical indifference.... Job avoided both of these dangers...."[83]

One more lesson emerges here from Job's journey of trials.

Lesson # 5: Trials have a way of revealing our view of God: What we believe about God and His character will mark our path moving forward.

Job's response to all of his calamities sounds unreal and a bit unbelievable at first:

"Shall we receive good from God, and shall we not receive evil?" (Job 2:10).

But you must admit that Job's response to his wife shows godly leadership and good stewardship. More importantly, it also reveals what he thinks about God in his suffering. His question positions Job as a faithful servant of God and demonstrates to us that God was right about Job and Satan was wrong. In fact, God tells us that all Job said about God was right (Job 42:7). If that statement does not make you want to go back and read the book of Job all over again, and note all the things Job said about God, then you are sleeping.

Job does not blame God nor does he "resign" from God's service

He reminds his wife that she has spoken foolishly and he corrects her thinking. His response is a literal confession of his confidence and trust in a God whose ways he does not understand.

Can we trust this giving God who is wise and knows best for us? Job believed you could, and thus he did not sin (Job 1:22; 2:10).

Randy Alcorn, in his book *If God Is Good* is quick to say,

> "What comes into our minds when we think about God is the most important thing about us. The most portentous fact about any man is not what he at a given time may say or do, but what he in his deep heart conceives God to be like..."[84]

Job models this sublime attitude toward God and that marks his stewardship as one that stands the test of time.

God Speaks—Again

Well, for Job it appears that the trial is over. The test is concluded. Yet life goes on. As the book continues there is this silence from heaven.

In all the intervening chapters only man talks to Job. Finally, from chapter 38 to chapter 42 we hear once again from God. Only in chapter 42 will we know that Job is vindicated. Blessing, not blight follow his severe testing.

> "The end comes at the end. The normal Christian life is warfare and waiting and being loved and humbled by God, and being justified by God, all in the here and now. But it is the expectation of blessing at the end."[85]

"Be patient, therefore, brothers, until the coming of the Lord. See how the farmer waits for the precious fruit of the earth, being patient about it, until it receives the early and the late rains....Behold, we consider those blessed who remained steadfast. You have heard of the steadfastness of Job, and you have seen the purpose of the Lord, how the Lord is compassionate and merciful" (James 5:7,11). When God is done with the matter, it comes out good (Romans 8:28).

"Better is the end of a thing than its beginning, and the patient in spirit is better than the proud in spirit" (Eccles. 7:8).

Job is an extreme book. He does not go from moderate riches to moderate poverty. He does not experience the loss of a job or the loss of one child. He loses everything in one day it seems.

Job's story is similar to our own on this earthly pilgrimage. Yet in the end, good stewardship is rewarded by grace. Job did not earn God's favor, but received it.

The Bottom Line

The bottom line in Job's trials is that he managed them as a good steward of God. You can summarize his management principles in three ways.

1: He allows himself to sorrow before God (Job 1:20a; Job 3; Eccles. 5:15).

2: He believes God is behind it all (Job 6:4; Isaiah 44:24–28; 45:9–10, 22–24; 46:8–10).

3: He counsels others with the comfort he himself received from the Lord (Job 2:9–10; 13:13–16; 19:23–27).

Considering these management principles a little more closely, we get a sense of what a good steward over trials looks like.

Job Sorrows

Job allows himself to sorrow before God (Job 1:20a; Job 3). Ecclesiastes 5:15 summarizes Job's experience well: "As he came from his mother's womb he shall go again, naked as he came, and shall take nothing for his toil that he may carry away in his hand."

Job is not a superman. Job learned that committed believers do not get a pass on trials. Trials *do* come to people who know and love the Lord.

His response to his trial is a natural one. Who among us has not sorrowed over some trial that has invaded our space, taken away our peace, and left us empty and depleted of any strength? Job's perspective is that life on earth will have its moments of trouble (Job 5:7), but God is there, witness to it all. God is not distant from His people if trouble overtakes them, even when He allowed it.

> *God is not distant from His people if trouble overtakes them, even when He allowed it.*

Job Believes

Job also believes God is behind it all. Job's view of God is a healthy one and a theologically correct one. It is also a very comforting view. God brings trial through various instruments, not to destroy us but to grow us. In Job's record we witness God taking up for the godly man and standing with the godly man. He gives and takes away – so the godly man can worship and bless God's name. (Job 1:20–21). Job understands that all his possessions and all his children were gifts from the Lord. Satan said Job would curse God, but he was wrong. Job blesses God. In his loss, his thoughts are on the God who gives and who, because He is God, in His wisdom has taken away. He does not blame God or walk away from his confidence in God (Job 1:22; 2:10b). Though he does not understand the reason for the trial and all that's behind it, he does believe God is good and can only give what His creatures can benefit from. That's why Job falls down and worships his God.

Dr. John Blanchard, noted preacher, teacher and apologist puts Job's worship response into perfect perspective:

> "None of us will ever be in circumstances in which there are no blessings for which God deserves thanks. Reeling from a personal tsunami in which he lost all his children and all his livestock, Job 'fell on the ground and worshipped,' crying, 'Blessed be the name of the Lord'" (Job 1:20–21).[86]

The Psalmist confirms this great reality. "The Lord is my Shepherd, I shall not want. He makes me lie down in green pastures. He leads me beside still waters. He restores my soul. He leads me in path of righteousness for his name's sake" (Ps. 23:1–4).

God cannot lead his sheep anyplace else but green, pastures, still waters, and right paths. It may not seem green or still or right at times, but God's name has been signed onto my trial.

God cannot lead his sheep anyplace else but green, pastures, still waters, and right paths. It may not seem green or still or right at times, but God's name has been signed onto my trial. Because He is a perfect God, sovereign in goodness and mercy, and because His name is on it, He cannot lead any other way. How sustaining is that truth! How encouraging is that biblical perspective! And how that reality energizes our faith and compels our worship of this Great and Mighty God!

Job Counsels

One more thing about Job's trial management should grip us. Notice what Job ends up doing in the midst of his trial (even when it comes to a close). He counsels others with the comfort he himself received from the Lord (Job 2:9–10; 13:13–16; 19:23–27).

What better place to start your counsel in trial than with your family—with those closest to you. It is easy to forget that Job's wife suffered along with him through all the losses and heartaches. She no doubt grieved and was on the verge of bitterness. What sweet counsel her husband gave her from his own faith and confidence in the one true God. We have received good from God and shall we not receive evil? In other words, Job was saying, though we don't understand all He is doing, we do know Him and can trust Him.

Job certainly did not waste his sorrows. He managed his trials like a good steward of God. And others were blessed by his responses. And we are among the blessed.

As we step back from Job's life of trial and think about how he stewarded his trials, we must make some careful decisions moving forward about our own trial management.

First of all, we must not allow ourselves to dwell too long on the "why" of the trial. I had a professor years ago in seminary who warned us that sometimes God is deliberately ambiguous. He would often say:

> "Students, you must be willing to let some things lay on the shelf that God chooses not to explain."[87]

My Dad's favorite verses that I heard him quote many times are a good reminder to me of how I must handle my own struggles with the "why" question.

"Oh, the depth of the riches both of the wisdom and knowledge of God. How unsearchable are his judgments and his ways past finding out. For who hath known the mind of the Lord? or who hath been his counsellor? Or who hath first given to him, and it shall be recompensed unto him again? For of him, and through him, and to him, are all things: to whom be glory forever. Amen" (Rom. 11:33–36, KJV).

> *Though the enemy thunders away like a lion, we need not be intimidated by the sound of his roar. When God says quiet, he has to be still.*

Do you believe God can be trusted with the "why" of your trial, even if He chooses never to explain it to you? Is God that wise and His decisions that reliable that you can rest on His love and grace toward you as His child?

Second, we must believe that the hand of God, though it moves, is never removed from my life. The hedge remains. The guard is always at the door.

"Little children, you are from God and have overcome them, for he who is in you is greater than he who is in the world" (1 John 4:4).

Satan is slippery, evil, and has great power, but he is held in check by the one who lives in me. The lesser is made to serve the Greater. The hand of God rules in my life over all. I am safe in the circumference and enclosure of that hand. Jesus said that I am held there in safety (John 10:28–30). Though the enemy thunders away like a lion, we need not be intimidated by the sound of his roar. When God says quiet, he has to be still.

Finally, pray that God would make your theology consistent with your practice. Nothing detracts from the Gospel more quickly and more assuredly than a believer who proclaims what he says he believes and then does not follow through with an everyday behavior that confirms that belief. Hypocrisy most often emerges when the "heat" of a trial comes on. If our confidence in God does not work in the midst of trials, and if what we say we believe is but window dressing displayed only on good days, then we have only a shallow faith at best. The power of the Gospel to a watching world is found in one who lives out its truth no matter what might be transpiring in his life.

The finality of our confession is this: The Word of God works because it is the Word of the living God. It will hold us and it will help us manage our trials as good stewards. Lean heavily upon its truth. It will not fail (1 Kings 8:56; Heb. 4:12).

Study Guide Questions

1. When trials come, one of the most human questions we ask is "Why?" What is good about asking that question and what can be unwise about raising that question? If you had the answer to that question would it change the way you think about the trial? Why or Why not? Wrestle with the issue of faith in terms of whether that question is answered or not? Would the way that question is answered increase your faith, or would it diminish your faith? Is faith crucial to trial management? In what way?

2. There is this idea floating around that if you do good things, good things will happen to you and if you do bad things, then bad things happen to you. How does Job's story refute that notion? What is the source of such thinking?

3. How does it comfort us to know that all of our trials must come through God's hand before they reach us? How does knowing that God may move the hedge but never remove the hedge help us persevere through our trials and manage them as good stewards?

4. None of us can navigate our trials alone. There are family members and friends that become engaged with us, whether we want them to or not. Do we have any responsibility to them in the midst of our suffering? What does stewardship have to do with our ministry to others? Consider Job's words to his wife in Job 2:9–10. She asked him a question and gave him a recommendation. What was wise about Job's answer? How did Job's answer show his care over his wife?

5. What is dangerous about the recommendation Job's wife gave him? How do we filter the advice we are given by friends and family in the midst of our trials? How can "bad" advice spoil the stewardship of our trials?

Conclusion

What's Next?

The "What's Next" chapter on this earth for all of us may include more of the same. Trials, troubles, disappointments, heartaches, and frustrations will no doubt come to us. And often we are reluctant to believe that anything good can result from them nor do we see how God can get any glory from these struggles of ours. James M. Boice in announcing to his congregation that he had been diagnosed with liver cancer in his last sermon to them said:

> "Should you pray for a miracle? Well, you're free to do that, of course. My general impression is that the God who is able to perform miracles—and certainly He can—is also able to keep you from getting the problem in the first place.... Above all, I would say pray for the glory of God. If you think of God glorifying Himself in history and you say, 'Where in all of history has God most glorified Himself?' the answer is that He did it at the cross of Jesus Christ, and it wasn't by delivering Jesus from the cross, though He could have...And yet that's where God is most glorified.... God is in charge. When

things like this come into our lives, they are not accidental. It's not as if God somehow forgot what was going on, and something bad slipped by.... God is not only the one who is in charge; God is also good. Everything He does is good.... If God does something in your life, would you change it? If you'd change it, you'd make it worse. It wouldn't be as good."[88]

Yes, God is good and He is the one in charge of our trials. But God has reminded us that all of these trials are but temporary. Peter tells us they are for a little while (1 Pet. 1:6).

By the grace of God and with the empowering of the indwelling Spirit of God they can be managed and triumphed over.

Someday there will be an accounting of our management of all of life, including our trials (2 Cor. 10). Yet God, in faithfulness, has promised to never, ever leave us (Heb. 13:5). He has promised his grace (Heb. 4:16) and his strength to us in abundant measure (Col. 1:11; 1 Pet. 1:5).

Peter reminds us that "His divine power has granted to us all things that pertain to life and godliness through the knowledge of him who called us to his own glory and excellence" (2 Pet. 1:3).

We have learned that for the various trials we face there is a corresponding "grace of God" given to exactly match the trial (remember that the word *various* means "many-colored"). There are some black-dark trials and some lighter-hued trials mixed into our experiences (1 Pet. 4:10). Therefore, we are given this grace to draw on, rest in and, yes, steward for His glory.

David Powlison in his book *God's Grace in your Suffering*, wisely counsels:

"God retains the right to work in ways beyond our comprehension. Because learning how to live is the most complex skill imaginable, the struggle will not cease until I have faced the last enemy and seen the face of God.... The Lord knows you. This reality is the single most important thing about you. You are his. This truth makes the decisive difference in how you walk down hard roads."[89]

The best way I know to wrap up our thinking on trial management comes from Peter's words:

"Beloved, do not be surprised at the fiery trial when it comes upon you to test you, as though something strange were happening to you. But rejoice insofar as you share Christ's sufferings, that you may also rejoice and be glad when his glory is revealed. If you are insulted for the name of Christ, you are blessed, because the Spirit of glory and of God rests upon you. But let none of you suffer as a murderer or a thief or an evildoer or as a meddler. Yet if anyone suffers as a Christian, let him not be ashamed, but let him glorify God in that name. For it is time for judgment to begin at the household of God; and if it begins with us, what will be the outcome for those who do not obey the gospel of God? And 'If the righteous is scarcely saved, what will become of the ungodly and the sinner?' Therefore let those who suffer according to God's will entrust their souls to a faithful Creator while doing good" (1 Pet. 4:12–19).

Once again we meet our "friend" stewardship. Peter admonishes us that when we suffer according to God's will we are to "entrust our souls to a faithful Creator while doing good."

As the old saying goes you can take these words "to the bank." Trials will come, but we have been graciously equipped to manage "God's property" for His glory and our good. When we learn to manage our trials as God's property, the blessing comes and the blight goes away. Don't fear the trials when they come. It is our opportunity to glorify God by good stewardship. And He will see us through.

John Piper once quoted an old hymn by Paul Gerhardt which seems an appropriate close to our consideration of trial stewardship. It is called "Give to the Winds Thy Fears."

Give to the winds thy fears,
Hope and be undismayed.
God hears thy sighs and counts thy tears,
God shall lift up thy head

Through waves and clouds and storms,
He gently clears thy way;
Wait thou His time; so shall this night
Soon end in joyous day.

Far, far above thy thought,
His counsel shall appear,
When fully He the work hath wrought,
That caused thy needless fear.

Leave to His sovereign sway,
To choose and to command;
So shalt thou, wondering, own that way,
How wise, how strong his hand.[90]

Endgame

Kindlings for Trial Stewards[91]

"The view of trials as a necessary medicine suited to our disease — powerfully reconciles us unto every cross. Everything is necessary, which God sends. Nothing is necessary, which God withholds."

—John Newton

"God does not send us two classes of providences—one good, and one evil. All are good. Affliction is God's goodness in the seed. It takes time for a seed to grow and to develop into fruitfulness. Many of the best things of our lives—come to us first as pain, suffering, earthly loss or disappointment—black seeds without beauty—but afterward they grow into the rich harvest of righteousness."

—J. R. Miller

"Will it not be good, if your present adversity results in the dethronement of some worshiped idol; in the endearing of Christ to your soul; in the closer conformity of your mind to God's image; in the purification of your heart; in a revival of God's work within you?"

—Octavius Winslow

"Affliction must not therefore be received as a burden, laid on by a blind and cruel fate—it is given by my wise and loving Father. Nor must I regard it as a "misfortune"—as an unmixed evil, which comes by chance, and is to be received with unconcern. Affliction does not come forth from the dust—it is from God. It is sent in mercy and wisdom—yes, and in power."

—Walter Purton

"So that no one would be disturbed by these afflictions; for you yourselves know that we have been destined for this" (1 Thess. 3:3).

"Not a pang can pierce the heart of His redeemed child, for which there is not a needs-be. Not an ache can gnaw the frame; not a grief can pierce the heart; not a shadow can darken the soul—which is not permitted because there was a needs-be. Admit for one moment, that CHANCE is the parent of your troubles — that accident is the author of your bereavements—and what a gloomy place must this world be. What a sad heart must the mourner's be. What an unhappy man must the victim of trouble be. But when we know that the blow that strikes the heaviest, is from our Father's hand; that the sorrow that pierces the heart with the keenest agony, lay in His bosom before it received its mission to touch us—then surely it is a truth, 'I, even I, am He who comforts you.'"

—John Cumming

"But more particularly, the day of adversity is intended for our INSTRUCTION. The Lord's rod has a voice which speaks to us lessons of heavenly wisdom. Therefore, we are required "to hear the rod, and Him who has appointed it" (Micah 6:9). "The rod and reproof give wisdom." (Prov. 29:15.) It presents to our minds many of the same great truths which are declared in Scripture—but which we may have overlooked, or failed rightly to understand — until they were pressed on our attention, and made the matter of our personal experience in the day of trouble."

—James Buchanan

"God Almighty knows that we are often purged more in one hour by a good sound trial—than by a thousand manifestations of His love. Happy are you who have got into Christ's fire."

—George Whitfield

"Afflictions are needful to wean us from earth—and to induce us to aspire after Heaven. At death sin dies, and sorrow expires. Sin is the mother—and sorrow is the daughter. The mother and daughter die on one bed, and are buried in one grave."

—William Nicholson

"It is good to know that there is a coronation after affliction. It is the prelude to an eternal weight of glory. It is good to know that there is a limit to affliction. It is but for a moment—it has its appointed end. Not always will the war go on. Not always will the seas be tempest-driven. Not always will the rains descend and the fierce winds blow. God weighs and measures, bounds and ordains, my sorrows."

—Alexander Smellie

If joy is ours—it is to make us a greater blessing to others. If sorrow is ours — it is to bring out Christ's image in us more clearly. If our hopes are disappointed—it is because God has some better thing for us, than that which we so earnestly desire. If we are called to endure pain—it is because godly character can only be matured by affliction. If bereavement comes and we are left without the human arm we have always leaned upon—it is because there are elements of character in our life which never could be developed unless the human support were removed. If our burdens are heavy—it is because we grow best under burdens. If we suffer wrong—it is to teach us better the great lessons of meekness, patience and sweet temper.

—J. R. Miller

"God's people have no charter of exemption from trouble in this life. While the wicked are kept in sugar—the godly are often kept in brine."

—Thomas Watson

"Our mercies far outweigh our afflictions. For one affliction—we have a thousand mercies. The sea of God's mercy swallows up a few drops of affliction. When God puts His children to the school of the cross, He deals with them tenderly. He will not lay a giant's burden upon a child's back. Nor will He stretch the strings of the instrument too much, lest they should break. If God sees it good to strike with one hand—He will support with the other. Either He will make our faith stronger—or render the yoke lighter."

—Thomas Watson

"They (our trials) are not left to 'chance.' They are all carefully selected—and divinely directed. God refines His people, displays His grace, and fulfills His precious promises—in the furnace of affliction."

—James Smith

"Afflictions serve to quicken the spirit of devotion in us; and to rouse us from that formality and indifference which frequently attend a long course of ease and prosperity. We are constrained to seek God with sincerity and fervor, when His chastening hand is upon us, since we then feel our absolute need of that help and deliverance, which He alone can give us."

—John Fawcett

"All the difficulties of the present life are but like one rainy day — compared to an everlasting sunshine. To a believer, this sorrowful life is like one drop of grief, lost in a sea of glory — or one speck of rain, in a year of fair weather."

—Charles Spurgeon

None of us has any trouble in accepting the doctrine of God's sovereignty—as long as things go to our liking. We are perfectly satisfied to let God have His way—as long as He does not cross us. We all believe in His administration, and are ready to "vote God in as our governor" as long as our business thrives, and our crops are plentiful, and everyone around our own table is healthy and happy. As long as His mercies are poured out in sweet wine—we drink of them gladly. But as soon as the same cup begins to taste of wormwood—we push it away in disgust, or cry out piteously, 'Let this cup pass from me. Any other cup I would have swallowed—but not this one.' If God had only tried me with the loss of property, and spared my health—I could have borne it. Or if He had sent the sickness at some other time—I would not murmur so. Or if His blow had struck me somewhere else but in my most tender spot—I would not cry out so bitterly. In short, if God had only consulted me as to the medicine I should take, and as to which branch His pruning knife should lop off—I would have been perfectly submissive."

—Theodore Cuyler

"Not one of all my tears has been shed for nothing. Not one stroke of the rod has been unneeded—or might have been spared. Your heavenly Father loves you too much, and too tenderly—to bestow harsher correction than your case requires. Beware then of a morbid dwelling on self with its crosses and losses. Our blessings are always greater than our trials; and most assuredly always greater than we deserve. Everything outside of Hell is mercy."

—John MacDuff

"Madam, when you are come to the other side of the water, and have set down your foot on the shore of glorious eternity, and look back again to the waters and to your wearisome journey, and shall see in that clear glass of endless glory nearer to the bottom of God's wisdom, you shall then be forced to say, 'If God had done otherwise with me than He hath done, I had never come to the enjoying of His crown of glory.' It is your part now to believe, and suffer, hope, and wait on: for I protest in the presence of that all-discerning eye who knoweth what I write and what I think, that I would not want the sweet experience of the consolations of God for all the bitterness of affliction: nay, whether God come to his children with a rod or a crown, if He come Himself with it, it is well."[92]

-Samuel Rutherford

The Last Kindling

(A song by Annie Johnson Flint that my parents used to sing as a
duet in church)

God has not promised skies always blue,
Flower-strewn pathways all our lives through;
God has not promised, sun without rain,
Joy without sorrow, peace without pain.

God has not promised we shall not know
Toil and temptation, trouble and woe;
He has not told us, we shall not bear
Many a burden, many a care.

God has not promised smooth roads and wide,
Swift, easy travel, needing no guide;
Never a mountain, rocky and steep,
Never a river, turbid and deep.

But God has promised strength for the day,
Rest for the labor, light for the way,
Grace for the trials, help from above,
Unfailing kindness, undying love.

Bibliography

The Holy Bible: English Standard Version. Wheaton, IL.: Good News Publishers, 2001.

The Holy Bible: Kings James Version. Nashville, TN.: Thomas Nelson Publishers, 1984.

The Transformation Study Bible: New Living Translation. Colorado Springs, CO.: David C. Cook, 1996.

Hymns of Grace. Los Angeles, CA.: The Master's Seminary Press, 2015

Great Hymns of the Faith. Grand Rapids, MI.: Zondervan Corporation, 1968.

Achtemeier, Paul J. *1 Peter.* Minneapolis, MN.: Fortress Press, 1996.

Alden, Robert L. *Job.* Broadman & Holman Publishers, 1993.

Alleine, Richard. *The World Conquered by the Faithful Christian.* Grand Rapids, MI.: Soli Deo Gloria Publications, 1995.

Ash, Christopher. *Job: The Wisdom of the Cross.* Wheaton, IL.: Crossway, 2014. Quoted Charles Bridges.

Ash, Christopher. *Out of the Storm.* Vancouver, British Columbia: Regent College Publishing, 2004.

Ash, Christopher. *Where was God When That Happened?* North America: The Good Book Company, 2017.

Alcorn, Randy. *If God is Good*. Colorado Springs.CO.: Multnomah Books, 2009.

Beeke, Joel R. and Slachter, Terry D. *Encouragement for Today's Pastors: Help from the Puritans.* Grand Rapids, MI.: Reformation Heritage Books, 2013.

Beeke, Joel R. *Jehovah Shepherding His Sheep*. Grand Rapids, MI.: Reformation Heritage Books, 1997.

Billheimer, Paul E. *Don't Waste your Sorrows*. Fort Washington, PA.: Christian Literature Crusade, 1977.

Blanchard, John. "Gratefulness in Prayer," Tabletalk, Nov. 2019.

Boice, James M. Sermon, Tenth Presbyterian Church, Philadelphia, PA, May 7, 2000. Quoted by Randy Alcorn, *If God is Good* Colorado Springs, CO.: Multnomah Books, 2009.

Boice, James M. *Amazing Grace*. Wheaton, IL.: Tyndale House Publishers, 1993.

Bosch, Henry G. *Encyclopedia of 7700 Illustrations*, Paul Lee Tan, ed. Rockville, MD.: Assurance Publishers, 1979

Brooks, Thomas. *Precious Remedies Against Satan's Devices*. London, ENG.: The Banner of Truth Trust, 1968.

Bunyan, John. *Prayer*. Carlisle, PA.: The Banner of Truth Trust,1995.

Caryl, Joseph. *An Exposition of Job*. Evansville, IN.: Sovereign Grace Publishers, 1959.

Challies, Tim. Ala Carte blog dated January 6, 2020. Quoted Tessa Thompson.

Chambers, Oswald. *My Utmost for His Highest* New York, N.Y.: Dodd, Mead & Company, 1963.

Chandler, Matt (with David Roark). *Take Heart: Christian Courage in an Age of Unbelief.* The Good Book Company/The Village Church, 2018.

Clark, Elliot. *Evangelism as Exiles: Life on Mission as Strangers in our own Land.* The Gospel Coalition, 2019.

Clines, J. A. *Job* 1–20. Dallas, TX. Word Books Publisher, 1989.

Cole, Cameron. *Therefore I Have Hope.* Wheaton, IL.: Crossway, 2018.

Davis, Andrew M. *The Power of Christian Contentment: Finding Deeper, Richer Christ-centered Joy.* Grand Rapids, MI.: Baker Books, 2019.

Davis, Dale Ralph. *1 Samuel: Looking on the Heart.* Geanies House, G.B.: Christian Focus, 2007.

Davids, Peter. *Commentary on James.* Grand Rapids, MI.: William B. Eerdmans Publishing Company, 1982.

Durham, James. *Lectures on Job.* Dallas, TX.:Naphtali Press, 2003.

Elliot, Elizabeth. *These Strange Ashes.* Ann Arbor, MI.: Servant Publications (Vine Books), 1998.

Eswine, Zack. *Spurgeon's Sorrows: Realistic Hope for those who Suffer Depression.* Geanies House, Scotland, UK: Christian Focus Publications, 2014.

Freeman, John. *Hide or Seek:* Greensboro, N.C.: New Growth Press, 2014.

Frost, Gerhard E. *The Color of the Night: Reflections on the Book of Job.* Minneapolis, MN.: Augsburg Publishing House, 1977.

Furman, David. *Learning to Kiss the Wave.* Wheaton, IL.: Crossway, 2018.

Goldsworthy, Graeme. *Prayer and the Knowledge of God.* Leicester,ENG.:Inter-Varsity Press,2003.

Gordon, Edward. *Miracle on the River Kwai.* London, ENG.: 1963.

Green, William Henry. *The Argument of the Book of Job* (Minneapolis, MN.: James & Klock Christian Publishers, 1977.

Horton, Michael S. *A Place for Weakness.* Grand Rapids, MI.: Zondervan, 2006.

Hughes, R. Kent. *2 Corinthians: Power in Weakness* Wheaton, IL.: Crossway, 2006.

Hughes, Phillip. *2 Corinthians.* Grand Rapids, MI.: Eerdmans, 1962.

Kaiser, Walter C. *I Will Lift My Eyes Unto The Hills.* Wooster, OH.: Weaver Book Company, 2015.

Keller, Timothy. *Walking with God through Pain and Suffering.* New York, NY.: Dutton, 2013.

Kaung, Stephen. *The Splendor of His Ways.* (New York, NY.: Christian Fellowship Publishers, Inc.,1974.

Lewis, C.S. *A Grief Observed.* New York, NY.:HarperOne, 1961.

Lister, J. Ryan. *The Presence of God: Its Place in the Storyline of Scripture and the Story of our Lives.* Wheaton, IL.: Crossway, 2015.

Lockyer, Herbert. *Dark Threads the Weaver Needs: The Problem of Human Suffering.* Old Tappan, N.J.: Fleming H. Revell Company, 1979.

Longman, Tremper III *Job.* Grand Rapids, MI.: Baker Academic, 2012.

McCartney, Dan G. *James.* Grand Rapids, MI.: Baker Academic, 2009.

Meyer, F. B. *The Gift of Suffering.* Grand Rapids, MI.: Kregel Publications, 1991.

Montgomery, Leslie. *Redemptive Suffering: Lessons Learned from the Garden of Gethsemane.* Wheaton, IL.: Crossway Books, 2006.

Moo, Douglas J. *The Letter of James.* Grand Rapids: MI.: William B. Eerdmans Publishing Company, 2000.

Morgan, Robert J. *On This Day in Christian History.* Nashville, TN.: Thomas Nelson, 1997.

Morgan, Christopher W. and Peterson, Robert A. *Suffering and the Goodness of God.* Wheaton, IL.: Crossway Books, 2008.

Motyer, J. A. *The Message of James.* Downers Grove, IL.: Intervarsity Press, 1985.

Murray, Ian. H. D. Martyn-Lloyd Jones: *The Fight of Faith 1939–1981.* Edinburgh, ENG: Banner of Truth, 2004.

Naylor, Peter. *2 Corinthians vol. 1.* Auburn, MA.: Evangelical Press, 2002.

Parks, Joe. Horizons Stewardship, March 20, 2020 (https://us20.campaign-archive.com/?u=001faf6dc36451e1202183ef7&id=0ec43d11a3&e=fe5e0d8dd6)

Pershing, Betty ed. *Studies in Genesis and the Christian Life.* Glendale, CA.: G/L Publications, 1970.

Petty, James C. *Act of Grace: The Power of Generosity to Change Your Life, the Church and the World.* Phillipsburg, N.J.: P & R Publishing, 2019.

Piper, John. *A Sweet & Bitter Providence.* Wheaton, IL.: Crossway, 2010

Piper, John. *Future Grace.* Sisters, ORE.: Mulnomah Books, 1995.

Piper, John. *When The Darkness Will Not Lift.* Vereeniging, R.S.A.: Christian Art Publishers, 2008.

Powlison, David. *God's Grace In Your Suffering*. Wheaton, IL.: Crossway, 2018.

Powlison, David. *Safe & Sound: Standing Firm in Spiritual Battles*. Greensboro: NC.; New Growth Press, 2019.

Powlison, David. *Seeing With New Eyes: Counseling and the Human Condition Through the Lens of Scripture*. Phillipsburg, N.J.: P & R Publishing, 2003.

Reeves, Michael. *Rejoicing in Christ*. Downers Grove, IL.: IVP Academic, 2015.

Roper, David. *Teach Us to Number our Days*. Grand Rapids, MI.: Discovery House, 2008.

Rutherford, Samuel. *Letters of Samuel Rutherford*. Edinburg, Scotland.: Banner of Truth, 2006.

Spurgeon, Charles. *Grace Triumphant*. Grand Rapids, MI.: Baker Book House, 1964.

Stanley, Andy. *How to be Rich*. Grand Rapids, MI.: Zondervan, 2013.

Stedman, Ray C. *Let God Be God: Life-Changing truths from the Book of Job*. Grand Rapids, MI.: Discovery House Publishers, 2007.

Thomas, Derek W.H. *Strength for the Weary*. Orlando, FL.: Reformation Trust, 2018.

Tozer, A. W. *The Knowledge of the Holy*. Crownhill, Milton Keynes: Authentic Media Limited, 2012.

Tripp, Paul David. *New Morning Mercies*. Wheaton, IL.: Crossway, 2014.

Tripp, Paul David. *A Shelter in the Time of Storm: Meditations on God and Trouble*. Wheaton, IL.: Crossway Books, 2009.

Vroegop, Mark. *Dark Clouds, Deep Mercy*. Wheaton, IL.: Crossway, 2019.

Watson, Thomas. *The Godly Man's Picture*. Carlisle, PA.: The Banner of Truth Trust, 1992.

Wiersbe, Warren. *Devotions for Encouragement & Maturity*. Colorado Springs, CO.: Honor Books, 2005.

Wiersbe, Warren. *On Being a Servant of God* Nashville,TN.:Thomas Nelson Publishers,1993.

Wiersbe, Warren. *The Bible Exposition Commentary vol. 2.* Wheaton, IL.: Victor Books 1989.

Wiersbe, Warren. *The Bible Exposition Commentary: Old Testament History*. Colorado Springs, CO.: Cook Communications Ministries, 2003.

Zuck, Roy B. ed. *Sitting with Job: Selected Studies on the Book of Job*. Grand Rapids, MI.: Baker Book House, 1992.

Endnotes

Introduction

1   Robert J. Morgan, *On This Day in Christian History* (Nashville: Thomas Nelson, 1997), Feb. 11, 1917

2   C. S. Lewis, *A Grief Observed* (New York: HarperOne, 1961), 33

Chapter One

3   Keller, Timothy, *Walking with God through Pain and Suffering* (New York: Dutton, 2013), 13.

4   Leslie Montgomery, *Redemptive Suffering: Lessons Learned from the Garden of Gethsemane* (Wheaton: Crossway Books, 2006), 25

5   John Freeman, *Hide or Seek* (Greensboro: New Growth Press, 2014), 24–25

6   From Goodreads.com/quotes/44702 (website)

7   Warren Wiersbe, *Devotions for Encouragement & Maturity* (Colorado Spring: Honor Books, 2005), 25

8   Edward Judson, *Encyclopedia of 7700 Illustrations*, Paul Lee Tan, ed. (Rockville: Assurance Publishers, 1979), 1372.

9   Warren Wiersbe, *On Being a Servant of God* (Nashville: Oliver Nelson books), 70

10 F.B. Meyer, *The Gift of Suffering* (Grand Rapids: Kregel Publications, 1991), 31.

11 Henry G. Bosch, *Encyclopedia of 7700 Illustrations*, Paul Lee Tan, ed. (Rockville: Assurance Publishers, 1979), 1377.

12 J. A. Motyer, *The Message of James* (Downers Grove: Intervarsity Press, 1985) i J. A. Motyer, 38

13 Tim Challies in a recent blog (dated January 6th 2020) quoted Tessa Thompson

14 Andrew M. Davis, *The Power of Christian Contentment* (Grand Rapids: Baker Books, 2019), 139

15 ibid, J.A. Motyer, 38

16 D.L. Moody, ibid, *Encyclopedia of 7700 Illustrations*, pg. 524

Chapter Two

17 Paul David Tripp, *A Shelter in the time of Storm: Meditations on God and Trouble* (Wheaton: Crossway Books, 2009), 55

18 R. Kent Hughes, *II Corinthians: Power in Weakness* (Wheaton: Crossway, 2006), 92

19 ibid, R. Kent Hughes, 94

20 Cameron Cole, *Therefore I Have Hope* (Wheaton: Crossway, 2018) 111.

21 Warren Wiersbe, *Transformation Study Bible* (Ontario: David C. Cook, 1996), 1962

22 Philip Hughes, *II Corinthians* (Grand Rapids: Eerdmans, 1962), 451

23 ibid, R. Kent Hughes, 92

24 Joel R. Beeke and Terry D. Slachter, *Encouragement for Today's Pastors: Help from the Puritans* (Grand Rapids: Reformation Heritage Books, 2013), 160–161 (Quoted from Burgess, Scripture Directory).

25 Peter Naylor, II Corinthians vol. 1 (Auburn: Evangelical Press, 2002), 202

26 ibid, Peter Naylor, 203

27 David Powlison, *God's Grace In Your Suffering* (Wheaton: Crossway, 2018), 91

28 ibid, Warren Wiersbe, *Transformation Study Bible*,1963

29 Source unknown

30 ibid, Paul Lee Tan, ed. *Encyclopedia of 7700 Illustrations*, 1508–1509

31 ibid, Warren Wiersbe, *Transformation Study Bible*, 1963

32 Elliot Clark, *Evangelism as Exiles: Life on Mission as Strangers in our own Land* (The Gospel Coalition, 2019), 36–37 (Quoted from Peter Randolph, From Slave Cabin to Pulpit: The Autobiography of Peter Randolph)

33 Copied this several years ago from a sermon posted on the website "Ray Stedman. org/complete=library."

34 Source unknown

35 Colin Smith, *Unlocking the Bible Story vol. 4* (Chicago: Moody Press, 2002) pg. 159. (adapted by Kevin Halloran, on the web site Unlocking the Bible, August 30, 2016).

36 Banning Liebscher, blog article from Pastor to Pastor, June 18, 2020 (Pastor 2 Pastor churchsource@e.harpercollinschristian.com)

37 [37] David Powlison, *Seeing With New Eyes: Counseling and the Human Condition Through the Lens of Scripture* (Phillipsburg: P & R Publishing, 2003), 36

Chapter Three

38 [38] Paul David Tripp, *New Morning Mercies* (Wheaton: Crossway, 2014) Feb. 12

39 [39] ibid, Paul David Tripp, Feb. 12

40 [40] ibid, Paul David Tripp, Feb. 12

41 [41] Richard Wurmbrand, *Tortured for Christ* (New York: Bantam, 1977) 29

42 [42] J A. Motyer, Ibid, 34

43 [43] Andy Stanley, *How to be Rich* (Grand Rapids: Zondervan, 2013), 128

44 [44] ibid, Andy Stanley,129–130

45 [45] James M. Boice, *Amazing Grace* (Wheaton: Tyndale House Publishers, 1993), 203

46 [46] ibid, Andy Stanley,15

47 [47] ibid, Andy Stanley, 31

48 [48] ibid, Andy Stanley, 31

49 [49] ibid, Andy Stanley, 31

50 [50] *Hymns of Grace* (Los Angeles: The Master's Seminary Press, 2015),175

51 [51] Edward Gordon, *Miracle on the River Kwai* (London: 1963), 117

52 [52] ibid, Edward Gordon, 115

53 [53] Quoted from: John Piper, *Future Grace* (Sisters: Mulnomah Books, 1995), 256

54 [54] Joe Parks, Horizons Stewardship, March 20, 2020 (https://us20.campaign-archive.com/?u=001faf6d-c36451e1202183ef7&id=0ec43d11a3&e=fe5e0d8dd6)

55 [55] ibid, David Powlison, *Seeing with New Eyes* pg.53

56 [56] Warren Wiersbe, *Devotions for Encouragement & Maturity*, 37–38.

Chapter Four

57 [57] Source unknown

58 [58], Paul Lee Tan, ed. *Encyclopedia of 7700 Illustrations*, Quoted from the Sunday School Times (Rockville: Assurance Publishers, 1979), 404.

59 [59] C.S. Lewis, *Mere Christianity* (New York: Macmillan Publishing Co. Inc., 1981) 115

60 [60] Derek W. H. Thomas, *Strength for the Weary* (Orlando: Reformation Trust, 2018) 40

61 [61] Iain H. Murray, D.Martyn-Lloyd Jones: *The Fight of Faith* (Edinburgh: Banner of Truth, 2004), 387

62 [62] Principle Dr. John MacLeod quoted in ibid, Iain H. Murray, 65

63 [63] (I do not recall the article that suggested these thoughts. I jotted these down several years ago and I include them there because they were so helpful to me. My apologies to the unknown author).

64 [64] Oswald Chambers, My Utmost for His Highest (New York: Dodd, Mead & Company, 1963), 306

65 ⁶⁵ Ibid, Warren Wiersbe, *Devotions for Encouragement & Maturity*, 9–10

66 David Powlison, *God's Grace In Your Suffering* (Wheaton: Crossway, 2018), 91

67 ibid, Paul David Tripp, July 19

68 Michael Reeves, *Rejoicing in Christ* (Downers Grove: IVP Academic, 2015), 88, 98.

Chapter Five

69 From random reading, source unknown

70 John Piper, *A Sweet & Bitter Providence* (Wheaton: Crossway, 2010), 44

71 Dale Ralph Davis, *I Samuel: Looking on the Heart* (Ross-Shire: Christian Focus, 2007), 15

72 ibid, Dale Ralph Davis, 26

73 Warren Wiersbe, *The Bible Exposition Commentary: Old Testament History* (Colorado Springs: Cook Communications Ministries, 2003),209

74 *Great Hymns of the Faith*. (Grand Rapids: Zondervan Corporation,1968),361

Chapter Six

75 Christopher Ash, *Out of the Storm* (Vancouver: Regent College Publishing, 2004), 13

76 Charles Bridges, quoted by Christopher Ash, *Job: The Wisdom of the Cross* (Wheaton: Crossway, 2014), 32

77 (Copied from random reading over the past few years – source unknown)

78   David Powlison, *Safe & Sound: Standing Firm in Spiritual Battles* (Greensboro: New Growth Press, 2019), 15.

79   ibid, David Powlison, *Seeing With New Eyes: Counseling and the Human Condition Through the Lens of Scripture* , 47–48

80   ibid, Christopher Ash, *Out of the Storm* , 58

81   Stephen Kaung, *The Splendor of His Ways* (New York: Christian Fellowship Publishers, Inc.,1974),41

82   A.W. Tozer *The Knowledge of the Holy* (Milton Keynes: Authentic Media Limited, 2012), 129. Tozer rightly concludes that a right conception of God is basic not only to systematic theology but to practical Christian living as well. He says "The man who comes to a right belief about God is relieved of ten thousand temporal problems, for he sees at once that these have to do with matters which at the most cannot concern him for very long; but even if the multiple burdens of time may be lifted from him, the one mighty single burden of eternity begins to press down upon him with a weight more crushing than all the woes of the world piled one upon another. That mighty burden is his obligation to God. It includes an instant and lifelong duty to love God with every power of mind and soul, to obey Him perfectly, and to worship Him acceptably." pg.3

83   William Henry Green, *The Argument of the Book of Job* (Minneapolis: James & Klock Christian Publishers,1977),86

84   Randy Alcorn, *If God is Good* (Colorado Springs: Multnomah Books, 2009), 36

85   Ibid, Christopher Ash, *Out of the Storm*, 107

86   John Blanchard, "Gratefulness in Prayer," Tabletalk, Nov. 2019, pg. 27

87   Dr. John Lawler, Baptist Bible Seminary, Minor Prophets Class, 1998.

Conclusion

88 James Boice (sermon, Tenth Presbyterian Church, Philadelphia, PA, May 7, 2000), (quoted by Randy Alcorn, ibid, 15)

89 ibid, David Powlison, *God's Grace in your suffering*, 86, 33

90 Quoted from John Piper, *When The Darkness Will Not Lift*, (Vereeniging: Christian Art Publishers, 2008), 36–37. This was a quote by Paul Gerhardt from his hymn entitled: Give to the Winds Thy Fears (1656).

Endgame: Kindlings

91 Gleaned from Grace Gems (https://gracegems.org

92 Samuel Rutherford, *Letters of Samuel Rutherford* (Edinburg: Banner of Truth, 2006), 19. Rutherford wrote this letter to Lady Kenmure after the death of her second husband. She needed a note of comfort because she had previously lost her first husband and her brother as well as a child. Rutherford was able to comfort her by giving her an eternal perspective for the future because of his own trials. He himself buried two wives and all of his children with the exception of one daughter who survived him. He truly exhibited what it means to be a good steward of one's trials.